FAST W(

THE RISE OF
STEVE HARMISON

Tony Lawrence

Published in 2005 by
First Stone
A Division of Corpus Publishing Limited
PO Box 8, Lydney,
Gloucestershire GL15 6YD

ISBN 1 904439 43 8

Manufactured in Great Britain

10 9 8 7 6 5 4 3 2 1

To John and Jennifer.

ACKNOWLEDGEMENTS

Thanks to Brian Murgatroyd, Niall Edworthy and my wife Jan for help and advice. Thanks to everybody else who offered me their time and much-valued thoughts.

ABOUT THE AUTHOR

Bristol-born Tony Lawrence has spent the bulk of his 20-year career in journalism with two of the world's largest agencies, Agence France Presse and Reuters. His work in news and sport has taken him around the world, covering such diverse events as an Indian general election, Mother Theresa's funeral, winter and summer Olympics and a string of major championships, including cricket and rugby World Cups.

CONTENTS

CHAPTER ONE

LAUGHTER AT LILAC HILL

Uncertainty. Respect. Fear. These are elements a tearaway fast bowler might hope to impress on opponents at the start of an Ashes tour. But at Lilac Hill in 2002, in the Ashes curtain-raiser against the Australian Cricket Board Chairman's XI, all Steve Harmison could induce was laughter.

The match began badly for the gangly young man from Durham, and rapidly fell away. Fielding in the deep, he tripped over his own legs and suffered concussion as he nose-dived to the ground. But if England's novice fast bowler had counted on a sliver of sympathy from the Lilac Hill crowd as he struggled to regain his senses, he was quickly disabused. Thrown the ball by Nasser Hussain, he soon embarked on as wayward an over as he would ever bowl.

Striving for pace while battling with nerves, he speared his first ball wide down the leg side, followed by a second, then a third. When Harmison's next ball hurtled way out of the batsman's reach as well, prompting the umpire to signal to the scorers yet again, the cheers turned to jeers, which in turn gathered into waves of laughter as a fifth, sixth and seventh successive delivery left wicket-keeper Alec Stewart sprawling miserably on the ground.

"The crowd were laughing hysterically," Malcolm Conn, cricket correspondent with *The Australian* newspaper, recalls. "It was just fantastic sport, sticking it up the poor old Poms. I had been writing some pretty disparaging, condescending stuff, just the sort I like writing every time an Ashes series comes around.

"Then they get out to Lilac Hill and this kid is running around like a six-month-old Labrador. He keeps whacking his ears with his legs and concusses himself on the field, and then can't hit the cut stuff. It was just another chapter of 'lampoon the Poms'. It was fantastic theatre, we absolutely lapped it up. We were even laughing in the press box."

Harmison, who had made his England debut just two months before, took 14 balls to finish the over, bowling eight wides in all. He bowled 16 in the match and, to Australian delight, England lost to a collection of greying veterans, journeymen and young prospects. Officially, the fixture was billed as no more than a friendly stretching of the legs at a pretty venue just outside Perth, Australia's one concession to the notion of a 'festival match' before the tour began in earnest. But, as Stewart points out: "As soon as you go to Australia there is no such thing as a friendly game."

The result, English embarrassment apart, may have mattered little, but England's captain was left wondering how the experience might affect his raw, ragged pace bowler. As if to underline his concern, the first jokes about his young charge had already begun to appear via next morning's press, the favourite soon established as: "What is the address of Steve Harmison's web site? Wwwwwww..."

What made matters worse was that Harmison, along with Welshman Simon Jones, had been talked up as a genuine threat on Australia's hard pitches. With question marks over the fitness of Darren Gough, one of the mainstays of the England attack, and with Australia desperate for a genuine contest after dominating the Ashes since the late 1980s, the two young strike bowlers found themselves attracting more attention than they perhaps merited. They had played just one Test each.

Jones's tour did not last beyond the opening afternoon of the First Test, as he ruptured a knee in excruciating circumstances while fielding in Brisbane. Harmison's trials in Australia were more psychological than physical. Within a few weeks of Lilac Hill, he underwent a much more significant ordeal in the Third Test in Perth. In front of a buoyant, baying Western Australian Cricket Association (WACA) crowd, Harmison lost his run-up and his rhythm so completely that, like a blind man groping his way down a narrow alley, he repeatedly struggled to get to the crease.

That was later. On October 22, 2002, a day before Harmison's 24th birthday, Hussain was more concerned with protecting someone who had already been caricatured as a gentle giant with an egg-shell personality. "I was trying to keep him optimistic. I didn't want him getting downbeat," Hussain said. The seven consecutive wides, in themselves, were irrelevant. Harmison's state of mind was what mattered. How would he respond when things really warmed up, in the harshest cricket environment of them all?

On August 22, 2004, Harmison became the world's top-ranked bowler. The honour came less than two years after he had lost his radar at Lilac Hill, and barely 10 months after England's selectors had met him face-to-face for a frank discussion over his commitment to the cause. It came five months after he had rocked West Indian cricket to the core.

The 6ft 4ins strike bowler had repaid the faith placed in him by so many and for so long by gate-crashing his way from back-of-house to centre stage with an epic spell of fast bowling at Sabina Park in Jamaica. West Indies were obliterated for 47, their lowest Test score of all time. One moment Harmison was just another English bowler, albeit an odd-ball with enormous potential, the next he found himself, according to the ratings, worthy of comparison with the likes of Glenn McGrath and Shane Warne. If Harmison found it hard to believe, then so did England's long-suffering cricket followers.

A month later even they, however, had begun to think the unthinkable – that at last England might have found a bowler to strike genuine fear into opponents – when Harmison's new-found status was confirmed with selection for the International Cricket Council's team of 2004. Suddenly his name appeared on a fantasy team sheet including such figures as Warne, Brian Lara, and Ricky Ponting. Harmison, well versed in the art of self-effacement, was quick to set his achievements in a less flattering context. He could not imagine that his new and transient world ranking would perturb any top-class batsman taking guard against him, he said. Real reputations were built over the long term, not over a single 'annus mirabilis'. Nor was he willing to accept that his talent could begin to be compared with that of Australia's McGrath, whom he considered the best fast bowler around.

His level-headed realism, however, could not mask a meteoric rise. Before his historic seven wickets for 12 runs in Jamaica, Harmison was barely known beyond the confines of Durham's Riverside stadium or, indeed, far outside his home town of Ashington. In nearby Newcastle, few would have turned and pointed as he loped anonymously down the street. Sabina Park and the West Indies tour, however, changed everything. "In the space of a few weeks, he became a sensation," said England's chairman of selectors, David Graveney. "He just reinvented himself."

It is tempting to root about for some magical key that unlocked Harmison's undoubted potential. Who was that one man, blessed with an alchemist's touch, who turned Northumberland coal into diamond? What was that single event which catapulted him from near-anonymity to stardom? Perhaps his rebirth as a cricketer was all built on a chance meeting, or some bizarre coincidence? The truth, though, is more prosaic. While David Graveney, England's chairman of selectors, happily highlights those he perceives as critical influences, he nevertheless believes that Harmison's success story has been pieced together gradually, with a wide cast contributing to the overall picture.

"The bottom line is, there are a lot of people who played their part. There's not one thing that you could say turned him around," says Graveney. "But in the end it has to be the bloke at the end of the run-up. He's the guy who's got to bowl the ball."

The fact that Harmison has indeed managed to bowl the ball, and with such devastating effect, seems little short of miraculous. The odds were not in his favour. Cricket was never his first love. Once, as a young man, he even made a concerted effort to cold-shoulder the game and follow another road. Even now, after a day's toil in England colours, you sometimes sense a reluctance in him, as if he would prefer to be elsewhere.

Many of his friends and colleagues see him as a sporting paradox. A home-town boy and a committed family man, he struggles with the peripatetic lifestyle of an international sportsman, glancing occasionally over his shoulder with envy at those burdened with more mundane, familiar routines. He enjoys the game but not his career. Nor has he ever craved the attention or, indeed, the rewards that his talent now attracts. It is as if fame sought him out, and not the other way around.

While his long-limbed frame and natural ability to propel a ball at high speed make him perfectly designed for cricket, his mentality seems better suited to working in a quiet corner of his local library. It would be no great surprise, indeed, if one day Harmison retreated from the bright lights as suddenly as he stepped into them. For him, the life of a world-class cricketer has never been, and probably never will be, a laughing matter.

CHAPTER TWO

'WOR JACKIE', BOBBY, AND PELE, TOO

Stephen James Harmison was born in Ashington on October 23, 1978.

There was no doubt, from the very beginning. He was destined to play football for Newcastle and England. It was written in the stars and suggested in his genes. The boy was born in the best of places and on the most auspicious of dates. The sporting gods could not have made their intentions more clear had Harmison arrived in the world with a black-and-white scarf wrapped about his neck and a football tucked under the arm.

Ashington lies in the north-east of England, around 15 miles north of Newcastle upon Tyne. It is a tough, Spartan, no-nonsense sort of town where, they say, people take five years to talk to outsiders, ten to trust them and 20 years to consider them as friends.

For much of its modern history, it had no claim to fame beyond coal. A hamlet made up of a few farms at the start of the nineteenth century, it was to mushroom into a thriving pit community as the industrial revolution took hold. "The world's biggest pit village" a plaque in the centre of town boasts, where 5,000 people, "pit yackers" as they were called locally, once worked the mines. For more than a century, its men, women and children fed off the colliery and the seams spreading out beneath the surrounding countryside. By the end of the 1980s, however, many of those jobs, as well as those in surrounding pits, had been exported by the Thatcher Government, the shafts boarded over and the gates locked, leaving a community to reinvent itself. Nearby Ellington colliery, the last pit in the north-east, was closed in February 2005.

Years before, one of Ashington's favourite sons escaped the clutches of the mines to find his fortune elsewhere. Jackie Milburn, 'Wor Jackie', played football for his beloved Newcastle United and for England during the 1940s and 50s. One of the sport's first superstars, he scored almost 250 goals for his club, a total yet to be surpassed. He was a family man, rooted in his local culture and suspicious of fame. But when he died in 1988, Newcastle came to a standstill in his honour. His ashes were scattered on the pitch at United's St James' Park ground. Statues were erected in his birthplace and in Newcastle. Every day, shoppers in Station Road in Ashington can look up at him as he controls a ball deftly on his left foot.

His nephews, Bobby and Jack, were also Ashington-born and destined for soccer greatness. The younger Charlton graced the red of Manchester United and Jack the white of Leeds. Both excelled for England and played together in the World Cup-winning side of 1966. Bobby survived the Munich air crash that decimated the Manchester United side of 1958 to win three league championships, the 1968 European Cup and to score a record 49 goals in 106 appearances for his country. 'Big Jack' – who always referred to Bobby as 'wor kid' – also flourished as a manager, leading Ireland to the 1990 World Cup quarter-finals.

Had things taken a different turn, England's World Cup triumph might have had an even stronger Ashington flavour. Jimmy Adamson, born in the town and one of Burnley's greatest players, was offered the England manager's job before the tournament but turned it down. Alf Ramsey said yes, and the rest is history.

Milburn, Adamson and the Charltons feature prominently in Ashington's imposing Woodhorn Colliery Museum. Harmison, as yet, does not.

As a boy, he dreamt of emulating them. When you share your birthday with Brazilian Pele, the greatest footballer of them all, you should be permitted such fantasies.

His father, no doubt, approved. Jimmy Harmison had been a fine player himself, excelling at semi-professional level with Blyth Spartans and Yeovil Town. There had even been talk of a professional career before he opted to return to the security of Northumberland.

Stephen certainly had an aptitude for football. What he lacked in explosive pace and nimbleness on the turn – a weakness shared by most of the soccer-obsessed Harmisons – he made up for with imposing stature and an ability to read the game. He soon settled for life as a bullying centre-back, while worshipping the striking exploits of Alan Shearer from afar.

He also had a gift for cricket. The family – which expanded to two brothers, both fine sportsmen, and a sister – still live on the edge of the cricket field. But this is committed football country, where even rugby World Cup winner Jonny Wilkinson is not deemed worthy of lacing Shearer's boots.

Durham had become England's 18th first-class cricket county at the end of 1991, just after Harmison's 13th birthday. But according to Ashington cricket club coach Steve Williams, a family friend, Steve was interested only in football. "He played for Northumberland schools, but we never saw any Harmisons at county net sessions because they were such good footballers. They are a very football-oriented family."

It was not until he was around 11 that Harmison began appearing at the cricket club. Even then, he was only really marking time before the start of the football season.

"He could already bowl. He had a lovely natural action which hasn't changed all that much. He had a bit about him," says Williams. "But he wasn't really way ahead early on. At under-13 and 15 level, he wasn't the best. He was quick but fairly erratic and tended to bowl too short."

At some stage during his teens it began to dawn on Harmison that, despite all the portents, he would never be good enough to earn a living at football. He was good enough for Ashington and the Northern League, but he would struggle to make much of an impact beyond.

"At 13 or 14 he played for East Northumberland. He was that much bigger than everybody, a giant compared to the rest of them, but at around 15 they started catching him up a bit. He wasn't knocking people off the ball as much," says Williams.

Having left school early without causing too many academic ripples – indeed, tall enough to get served a lager without challenge in the local pubs, he spent a portion of his final year playing truant – Harmison seemed ready to settle for his lot. Jimmy worked in a local factory while excelling as an amateur sportsman and his son, burdened with the quiet regrets of every Newcastle United season ticket holder, looked set to follow in his footsteps.

His cricketing talent, however, began to flower despite himself. "I thought he might do something if he really wanted it, but he was so laid back when he was younger. He wasn't hungry," Williams adds. "We had 100 kids at the cricket club and I used to say to them: 'I just wish I had his ability.' He was so laid back, he could be horizontal. I've known his dad for more than 30 years and I've known him since he was a dot. It was just the way he was.

"He's a lovely lad but he was always an old head on young shoulders. I always said he was 15 going on 21. He was streetwise, brought up in an adult environment, playing pool and listening to the men in the social club. He wasn't a know-it-all, but he wasn't going to come up and ask how to bowl away swingers. I never really coached him, I just let him bowl. I took him to matches. I was just his taxi driver, really."

Harmison, while playing for the county's youth sides alongside Williams' son Greg, did not even seem aware that cricket might offer a career. Nor, at that stage, had anybody taken much notice of him, least of all his own family, despite his promise. Cricket was largely played for fun. Once, five of the Harmisons – dad Jimmy, his two brothers Kevin and Melvyn, and sons Stephen and James – turned out for the same Ashington third XI.

Harmison and his friend Greg did win selection for Northumberland's junior cricket sides but they did not feel that they belonged. "There were lots of lads from the private schools. We stuck out like a sore thumb," says Greg. "The coach didn't have much time for us. Harmy was quick then, and used to like a banter with batsmen. He used to get fired up in those days. But he was all over the shop."

There had been a close encounter with one star in the making – as a youngster, Harmison played in a regional tournament, which included a highly rated England Under-15 player by the name of Andrew Flintoff – but the quiet boy from Ashington still had a lot of growing to do. When he did start to develop he caught everybody out, himself included.

Williams, a hospital engineer, remembers the sudden change of tempo very well. "It just happened between 16 and 17. He shot up, and got better and better. Up to then, he was no more than a good net bowler for us at the club. The practice wickets weren't that good, but he was a nice steady pace and he would bowl all night. That winter, I didn't get a lot of indoor nets because of my work shifts. The captain at the time came to me around April and said he wanted to play Stephen in the first team. I didn't think he was ready though, and said so.

"I had a net against him soon after. Stephen had grown about four inches to 6ft 2ins. He was also two yards quicker and had improved out of sight. He was rapid, and I mean rapid. He pinned me to the back wall. He pinned everybody there.

"After that, I always timed my batting practice, padding up just after Stephen – or High Towers, as he got nicknamed – had had a bat, so that he would want a breather and wouldn't be ready to bowl. I haven't faced his bowling since, nor do I want to."

Until then, indeed, one of Harmison's most impressive exploits had been as a batsman. "He and Greg still hold the league record of 225 runs for the first wicket," says Williams. "They opened the batting as under-15s in an under-17 league game. I put them in because a couple of older lads were late. They were away on work experience, so I just said, 'You two go in for a change.' Steve scored 143 and kept pulling sixes to square leg and into the old age pensioners' day centre."

The serious bowler, however, had now arrived and his reputation in club cricket spread quickly. His dreams may still have drifted towards St James' Park but his sporting achievements would increasingly be reserved for the Ashington cricket ground, with its unprepossessing pavilion and sagging far boundary, off Kennilworth Road near the town centre. Even after launching his professional career, Harmison turned out for his club when circumstances permitted.

Ashington Cricket Club had boasted a major star once before. Rohan Kanhai, one of the best West Indian batsmen of all time, was the club professional for a few years. To date, Kanhai is the one cricketer publicly immortalised in Ashington (although the Rohan Kanhai free house attempts to lure in customers with the promise of live televised soccer rather than cricket). For now, Harmison's recognition is less overt. While there are pictures of Kanhai at one end of the club pavilion, the other is fast becoming a shrine to the local prodigy, with signed England team pictures and shirts adorning the walls. His picture also hangs in the Royal Antediluvian Order of Buffaloes (RAOB) men's social club, frequented by the Harmisons, just down the road.

Greg, now the Ashington captain, remembers one 50-over game in particular during his friend's formative years. "It was against the County Club from Jesmond. They were one of the better teams. Steve had been at Durham for a couple of years by then. They batted first, as I remember, and were bowled out for 35. He got three wickets and Martin Pollard at the other end got seven, because they were all trying to get away from Steve. The keeper was standing way back. I don't think they were too impressed that Steve was playing."

Kieran McGrane, deputy head at Ashington High School, was also privileged to watch Harmison come of age. He joined the school as a PE teacher in September 1992, on the same day as the 13-year-old boy who would become one of his most outstanding students.

"He was always happiest in his PE lessons," says McGrane. "I think it would be safe to say that that is where his strengths lay. He was a very, very easy-going young man, nothing was too much trouble. Whereas he would sometimes get into a little bother in other lessons, he was totally charming, helpful and co-operative with me.

"My colleagues would say he wasn't interested or responsible, but I would tell them to come and watch him in my lessons. He stood out a mile. There are very few students that you come across at that age that you feel you can talk to on an adult level. Stephen was one. Treat him as an equal and he would respond in kind."

He also had a lung-burning stamina that would serve him well later. "If you did fitness or beep tests, Stephen would always be good. He would spend the day at school, then have a football match or training in the evening. I would go training at seven o'clock at night and there he would be, with Jimmy, doing the same work-out as the adults. I don't think at that age he would have seen it as hard work; it was more a case of him having fun while avoiding his homework."

Already he was a chip off the old block; cautiously shy, undemonstrative, keeping himself to himself. "Families in Ashington are still very male dominated and there's a particular caricature of what a male is. And Stephen fits that," says McGrane.

He was at his most vocal on the sports pitch. "His two main sports were football and cricket. He was captain of the school football team, a centre back just like his dad – not a great deal of pace but plenty of skill. He used to come and train with a semi-pro team I used to play for, Morpeth Town.

"His dad helped out there as well, so I saw a lot of him and you could tell as a junior that he read the game very well. His skill level was quite a bit above his contemporaries. He used to find it a bit difficult with me being a teacher: he used to call out 'Sir, Sir!' and the other players would give me a lot of hassle. It took him a long time before he would call me by my first name."

McGrane is a west-coast Scot, born near Kilmarnock. He, too, was brought up on a diet heavily laced with soccer. Cricket, in contrast, was a foreign language but when he got the job at Ashington High School he was put in charge of the team.

"When they told me, I thought: 'Oh my goodness, what am I doing?' But I soon sorted out a good system with Stephen. Effectively, he took charge of the team and told me that, as long as I came along and umpired, he'd sort out the batting order, the bowling and the field placings. All I needed to do, he said, was to turn up and stand in the middle. And that's exactly what happened. It's possibly been the easiest and best school team I have ever run in terms of a pleasant atmosphere. All the boys respected Stephen implicitly because of his talent. He didn't showboat, he took it seriously and the other boys responded, and I used to sit back and enjoy it. I have yet to find another boy who could quite do that."

McGrane may not have been a cricket aficionado "but I realised how good he was, without a shadow of a doubt. He just bowled one ball and you thought: 'Oh my goodness!' Watching him bowl at other boys, I used to pity them. I couldn't think of anything worse than facing his bowling, even at 14. He was very quick compared to the others, in a different league. It would be like him as he is now, playing against a club side. He would open the batting, routinely hit sixes and score 50 or 60 runs, and on occasions retire so that other people had a bat. Then he would bowl and take five or six wickets."

McGrane was intrigued to see that there were two quite distinct personalities emerging: the mild-mannered schoolboy suddenly transformed into something altogether more ruthless.

"I always remember a story Stephen told me when he was playing for Ashington against one of the Durham teams. He fired a delivery in at this batsman and it whistled past, or might even have hit him, and the batsman looked up, smiled and winked at him. And Stephen thought: 'You cheeky git.' So he hit him with the next two square in the chest, and the next ball got him out. And Stephen winked back as he was walking off.

"That kind of summed Stephen up. The thing that I found strange was that he didn't mind hitting people. He has that edge to him, which is not in the rest of his personality. I don't know if that's the competitive spirit coming out, but when he talked about that incident he saw nothing wrong with hitting the batsman; that was part of the deal. He wanted to get him worried and then take his wicket.

"But beyond the boundary he is totally laid back. I think if somebody says something to him, he internalises it, determined to get the better of them rather than responding verbally or losing his rag. That edge, I guess, is the difference between those who are top sportsmen and those who play club cricket."

Steve was not exactly a shrinking violet on the football pitch either, but then none of the Harmison clan was. The whole family played to a high level. Jimmy led the way but his brothers, Kevin and Mel, were also very good players. All were defenders, all six-footers. They played in a Sunday morning team called the Ashington Buffs. Invariably they won their league. Steve made the odd appearance, too.

"Then you almost had the Harmisons en masse," says McGrane. "It used to be that if you messed with one Harmison, you messed with them all. You just didn't do that. It was much better to be on their side. Jimmy and his brothers are hard men. They used to offer me a little protection as well so I used to like playing with them. But they're a smashing family and very straight down the line.

"They're very well known in Ashington. You can't possibly have been involved in football and cricket and not know the Harmisons."

Steve's adolescent dreams of a professional career, however, had faded by the time he left school. He left at the first opportunity. He had never enjoyed it. But there was no real plan B. Considering his lack of qualifications, he was left with few options.

"I don't think he knew what he wanted to do when he left," says McGrane. "He left at 16, went off working with his dad, and there was probably a year or two when he just thought: 'This is what my life is.' I might be wrong, but I don't think the thought of a cricket career really entered his head."

The sporting gods, though, had a few more tricks to play on him. They had given him a perfect background coupled with passion for football only to deny him the ability to live out that passion. Now they taunted him further by gifting him extraordinary physical attributes to excel at another game, which he admired rather than loved. On leaving school, Harmison was not the biggest in his class. That soon changed.

"He just shot up in size," says his former teacher. "I remember an early school team photograph and he was probably third or fourth tallest and even up to the age of 16 he wasn't noticeably taller.

"But from 16 to 19 he suddenly grew. His family lives close by and I used to bump into Stephen a lot, through the football or when he went to and from his mum's. I couldn't believe the size of him – he just accelerated up." It didn't particularly improve his football, but it was to take his cricket to another level.

McGrane sees less of Harmison now. He does not expect an official visit either. "He told me he would feel a hypocrite if he was invited back to some awards ceremony because he didn't really like school, so why go back in and tell kids that he really wanted to stick in and do it? But he did say that if he was around and we wanted him to do something sports-wise, like a cricket session, he would be happy doing that – that's the environment that he's comfortable with."

But he sees enough of England's strike bowler to know that he has barely changed despite his success. "He is well known here and I think people value the fact that he is not trying to be something that he is not. Anyway, the immediate response would be: 'Don't forget, we know where you have come from.' He would never leave himself open to that accusation.

"Ashington is not the kind of place where you try to lord it over others. You are what you are and you get your round in, like anybody else. Anyway, his mum and dad would not countenance any kind of showmanship. Jimmy wouldn't be into that at all."

To one side of McGrane's office hangs a signed Newcastle shirt in a frame. On the other there is a signed Harmison shirt, from his Durham days. McGrane, who also taught Steve's brothers Ben (an England Under-19 batting all-rounder of huge promise and, many say, of more natural talent) and James (a Northumberland cricketer and semi-professional footballer), asked for the shirt and it turned up almost immediately.

"While I had a very good relationship with him, probably better than most, I wouldn't regard myself as having been a confidant," he concludes. "But I cherish the fact that I taught him. The thing that I like about him is that whenever I bump into him, he's always very pleasant, I know that I can talk to him. I think that speaks volumes for him.

"I'm sure other teachers have had people who have gone on to better things and they quite reasonably forget anybody that they have met on the way up. I have had nothing whatsoever to do with Stephen's success but it's just nice to know you've had somebody through your hands who has gone on to absolutely brilliant things."

CHAPTER THREE

GAMBLING ON A GANGLY GEORDIE

In 1989, Durham decided to apply for first-class status. Harmison, approaching his eleventh birthday, was probably too busy kicking footballs against brick walls with his friends to notice. Without that decision, however, which would come to fruition three years later, he might never have been heard of.

Geoff Cook, the former Northants batsman, arrived at Durham in 1991 as director of cricket to oversee the transition from minor to major county. Middlesbrough-born, he was familiar with the area but found himself facing a dauntingly blank canvas. The club would not even have a permanent home for another four years.

"The set-up was very piecemeal," Cook says. "We signed a lot of big-name players coming to the end of their careers to get us over the first two or three years. We were always going to have to develop a strong youth system to get players for the next generation or two.

"I knew cricket in the area. We had played Durham as a minor county for a few years, but we had to find grounds which were going to be first-class venues, as well as people to run the club. It was a multi-faceted task, really."

Durham's initial band of ageing mercenaries was led by the likes of Ian Botham, Wayne Larkins and Australian Dean Jones, with future England chairman of selectors David Graveney as the first captain. Botham, once one of the world's great all-rounders and most dramatic of match-winners, was winding down. He managed to play a couple of Tests as a Durham player in 1992 but, in truth, his glorious 102-Test career for England had been on the slide since 1989. He, like Larkins and Jones, would have his moments – including a century on debut – but they were little more than short-term draw cards. Botham would only last a season and a half under the Durham standard. Larkins, at 38, was a couple of years his senior while Jones had crossed 30.

The county's future would rely much more heavily on local talent. Cook, working flat out to establish the club, had spent much of the preparatory year forging as many cricketing alliances as he could as he looked to the long term. "It was essential to make immediate contact with the local clubs. We looked at all the young players in the area in 1991, from the age of 16 up to mid-20s," he said. "Three or four of them joined us on full-time contracts. During that final year as a minor county we used about 30 players, bringing in people for trials."

The first signs were less than encouraging. "The Durham and north-east talent is legendary," says Cook. But the area had never matched the production lines of neighbouring Yorkshire, where it was once said you need only whistle down the nearest coal mine and a strapping fast bowler would emerge. In Durham, those aspiring to greater things knew they would have to pack their bags and market themselves further afield.

"When you analyse it closely, a lot of people have left this area, to join the Lord's ground staff and other counties, but not a lot, proportionately, made it to the highest level. So when we had trials I thought: 'There's not an awful lot coming through here.' I realised then that a lot of work had to be done to bolster the next generation. That's when the stark reality of the job came through."

Colin Milburn had been one of Durham's past success stories.

Born in Burnopfield, another mining village just south of Newcastle, during the Second World War, he impressed as a schoolboy before moving to Chester-le-Street in search of stronger opposition. A man mountain of prodigious power, his batting exploits at minor county level soon attracted Northamptonshire and England, only for his international career to be cut short by a car accident, which cost him an eye.

Tom Graveney, a right-handed batsman destined for greatness, was another north-eastern gem who found his way to the surface. Born even closer to Ashington, some 20 miles away in the village of Riding Mill, in the late 1920s, he would average more than 44 in 79 Tests. He made his name, however, at the opposite end of the country, in Gloucestershire. There would also be stints for Worcestershire and Queensland. The closest Graveney would get to contributing to the region of his birth would be through watching his nephew David completing his career as Durham captain.

The lack of exciting local talent was not Cook's only headache. Just as Durham were limbering up that year, Yorkshire were abandoning their stringent policy of only selecting players born within the county boundary. To underline their new approach, they went all the way to Bombay to recruit Sachin Tendulkar as their first overseas signing. Thus a likely lad from Durham or Northumberland – or indeed from Manchester, where future England captain Michael Vaughan was born before his parents crossed the Pennines – would now be welcomed with open arms just down the road at Headingley.

Cook, however, was having some successes. He also sought to re-launch players who had failed to make their mark elsewhere. Left-arm quick bowler Simon Brown was an obvious target since he was Durham-born. He had set off for Northants in 1987 but, starved of opportunities, was enticed home and earned an England cap before injuries and the heavy responsibility of carrying a young bowling attack began to take their toll. His success suggested there might be more diamonds to be discovered, if only Durham dug deep enough.

Steve Harmison was the subject of two blind-card gambles in 1996. Neither of them, the first just before his eighteenth birthday and the second just after, paid off. The results, indeed, were so emphatically unsuccessful that the traumatised teenager almost ended his association with the first-class game before it had really begun.

Durham gave him his debut in mid-September. England's Under-19 selectors quickly followed suit, calling him up to tour Pakistan at the end of the year. Durham had begun the season, their fifth as a first-class county, knowing nothing about him at all. It was as if he had appeared from thin air. By now, the county was well into the second phase of its development plan. Botham and company had proved as valuable for their publicity as for their playing exploits, indeed perhaps more so, but had gradually hobbled off into the sunset. The team was still struggling, however, and, despite localised successes, remained reliant on imports. Cook realised he would have to cast his net wider and began looking further north.

One day, out of the blue, he took a phone call from a contact who had seen a Northumberland Under-17s game. A tall pace bowler had stood out. "I think he might be worth a look," he had said. Cook, as he had done often before, set off on a scouting mission having scribbled down the name: Stephen James Harmison.

"I knew immediately, as soon as I saw him bowl," he recalls.

"He was then as he is now. He was very much his own type of bowler, all arms and legs and with his big leap in the delivery stride. He was gangly and bowled the ball on a natural length. He just looked a bowler, not somebody who was manufactured. It was very natural for him.

"He got to the wicket very easily, even if he sometimes looked a bit uncoordinated. I don't remember if he got any wickets against Durham Under-17s. I remember we won the game and I also remember saying to our youth development officer, Martin Robinson: 'There's a proper bowler on this pitch.' We just developed it from there. I think I spoke to him on the day and asked him if he would like to be connected with Durham."

Cook also watched Harmison play for Ashington before talking to Durham coach Norman Gifford, who would be as impressed. "We selected him for a couple of trial games. I saw him play a second XI match against Middlesex in South Shields," said Gifford, the former England spinner. "It was an interesting wicket, in that it had a little ridge in it – if you hit the upside, the ball flew, and if you hit the downside, it shot through. When you saw this kid run in and bowl you thought: 'Christ, this is a bit different from any of the others!' And he got wickets, five or six. He got bounce, even without the aid of the ridge. He was tall and bowled his height. Yes, he was raw and leaning away, his head was going out a bit, but what he did was special."

Cook adds: "Ian Gould was their coach and Stephen, I think, got nine wickets in the match and bowled absolutely beautifully – accurately, quickly and a super length. He came against better batsmen, which always turns him on, so probably his concentration levels were a bit higher. Now, where he pitched the ball, better batsmen were getting edges where in youth cricket that hadn't happened. Gould was absolutely overwhelmed."

Cook himself was delighted with his find but knew there was work to do. "I think there's every chance that we would not have heard of Steve Harmison if Durham had not got first-class status," he says. "Firstly, I don't think he would have been interested if another county had spotted him – he wouldn't have been keen on spending time away from Ashington. It would have been like playing away on a permanent basis. Secondly, at the age of 16 or 17, his performances weren't that exciting. The potential was there to see but he wasn't pulling up any trees.

"Our commitment to younger players was perfect for him. He still talks about how Durham treat their young players. Certainly Steve would have found it easier to integrate here."

Harmison found himself being asked to integrate much faster than he might have imagined. Yet to turn 18, he was given his county debut within a few months after being invited to the Durham Academy. Martin Saggers, an import from Norfolk who would also go on to play for England, had twisted an ankle while playing golf and the emergency call went out.

As baptisms of fire go, his would be hot enough to leave scorch marks. Durham, captained by Mike Roseberry with former England batsman John Morris (and Harmison's future agent) at his side, were hosting champions elect Leicestershire at their impressive new Riverside ground at Chester-le-Street in the death throes of the season.

"Resources were low, the team had had a poor year to put it mildly," Cook recalls. "Stephen had shown his potential so we pitched him in. Leicestershire were playing really positive, aggressive cricket – they were almost trend-setters in county cricket, in the way they were scoring and the pace they played the game, and Stephen was exposed to this. They showed no mercy."

Durham won the toss and opted to face a strong pace attack

led by Allan Mullally and David Millns. The damage, however, was done by West Indian Phil Simmons, who took extraordinary figures of six for 16 as the home side were routed for 146. Harmison helped put on a creditable 25 with Brown before being last man out, but he must have been unnerved by the sense of shock in the Durham changing room that September day.

Worse was to come. Simmons, a *Wisden* player of the year, carried on with the bat where he had left off with the ball as he hammered 171 off 170 balls, including 104 in boundaries, out of Leicestershire's 516 for six declared.

Harmison's nine overs went for 77 as he was carted to all parts without taking a wicket. He was not the only bowler to suffer at the hands of the Trinidadian, but he suffered the most. As a young man, Simmons had almost died after being struck on the head by England quick bowler David Lawrence. His heart stopped and he only recovered after emergency brain surgery. The mature Simmons, however, looked Durham's young pretender straight in the eye and made mincemeat of him. The 251-run humiliation was completed when Mullally took five wickets to skittle Durham for 139 in the second innings.

Northern Echo sports writer Tim Wellock remembers: "It was difficult for Steve, but he did look like a fish out of water. It wouldn't have been a surprise if he had never been seen again."

Cook, though, was less concerned. "He didn't bowl as well as he had in the second team. Whether it was the occasion, I don't know. It wasn't a disaster by any stretch. We had done it with a hundred lads before – Paul Collingwood was playing league cricket and suddenly he was opening the Durham batting. We were at that stage where we had to put people in, so we were used to that reaction, some came through okay and some took a little longer. But to say it was an eye opener is a bit of an understatement. After terrorising batsmen at a lower level, he realised then that there were some serious cricketers out there. He was disappointed of course, but he was fine. It was the last game of the season and he had a chance to go away and think about it."

Had the Leicestershire game taken place a couple of days earlier, England's Under-19 selectors might have given Harmison a wider berth. By chance, however, their squad selection meeting for the winter tour to Pakistan coincided with the mis-match at Chester-le-Street.

Micky Stewart, working as England's Director of Coaching and Excellence after running the full national team, chuckles at the memory.

"We met at Lilleshall. We had gone through the names of the players we knew when Geoff Arnold, who was the bowling coach, said there was this lad Harmison who had just suddenly appeared from nowhere. He said he was quick and very, very raw. He had played very little cricket but he was big and tall. The other name suggested was Dimitri Mascarenas, a medium-pacer. Harmison was making his Durham debut on that very day while Mascarenas was playing for Hampshire. I said we were looking for a breakthrough bowler – in Pakistan we would need something different, with the new ball not lasting too long.

"I told Geoff and John Abrahams that it was down to them because I had never seen Harmison. Geoff went for Harmison. The next morning in the paper I read that Harmison had been caned while Mascarenas had taken something like four for 40-odd. So I did pull Horse's [Arnold's] leg."

For Stewart, taking Harmison was a gamble. Arnold, however, a former England quick bowler himself, never saw it as a risk. "I just knew he had something," he recalls. "He used to bowl wide of the crease, pushing the ball in, but he also had the ability to hold the ball up. Bob Willis did something similar. I wanted him to go and I said it. I'm a fairly trustworthy bloke."

Abrahams agrees. "Geoff wasn't prone to making rash statements. He was so adamant that this lad was special that we felt we would be silly not to take him. It was just about recognising raw pace and seeing if the potential could be harnessed."

Within a short space of time, however, the decision to opt for Harmison would seem, at best, premature. Stewart flew out late to Pakistan to monitor the team's progress. By the time he arrived Harmison had already returned home.

Micky Stewart got his first look at Harmison when the England squad tuned up for the Pakistan trip at the National Sports Centre at Lilleshall. Like everybody else, he liked what he saw, even if he couldn't quite describe it. In those days, Harmison rocked from side to side like a yacht caught in a squall, his elbows swinging to port and starboard as he tacked towards the crease before taking a huge leap in his delivery stride and releasing the ball in a whirl of arms and legs.

Stewart said: "He looked a bit like a praying mantis, going in all directions, arms, legs and feet. But it was obvious what Horse meant."

He also quickly made an impression on his team-mates-to-be. "Lilleshall is quite conducive to fast bowlers anyway," explains Abrahams. "The indoor nets are quite skiddy and hard so I wasn't too popular every time I put somebody in his net."

It soon became apparent, though, that the 18-year-old, who came across as shy and difficult to engage in conversation, was having greater difficulty in finding his feet away from training. Many of the other players were already well-travelled England veterans, as well as good friends. The gregarious Flintoff was the centre of attention, with fellow all-rounder Ben Hollioake and pace bowler Alex Tudor equally confident. Wicket-keeper Chris Read and spinner Gareth Batty were also present and destined for greater things.

"For an Under-19 side we were quite experienced and there were some strong characters," adds Abrahams. "There were quite a number of boys who had been through the system whereas Steve was completely new to it. On a tour to Pakistan there isn't much social life, so you have to bond as a team, which is both a help and a hindrance."

Durham coach Gifford had joined Arnold during one training stint at Lilleshall but the addition of a friendly face did not make things any easier. "Giff and I were there but Steve wasn't very happy staying at Lilleshall. We were there for three or four days and he wasn't happy doing that," says Arnold. "Being away from his family and his environment, he just struggled. He didn't really want to know.

"In those days he didn't say much anyway, he just got on with his bowling. There were a couple of times when Giff and I had a chat with him in his room. It was like getting blood out of a stone."

Harmison's solid work ethic during the training sessions probably helped mask the problems that he would face in Pakistan. Even then, he might have succeeded in adapting to his new situation and surroundings but for an early back injury that was to compound his sense of isolation on the sidelines.

"It's not the easiest tour to go on, and for a youngster with his lack of experience in travelling, in England let alone abroad, he was homesick," Abrahams says. "It was quite common. In Pakistan you got up early and the matches were over by five o'clock. There was a lot of time at the hotel with little to do."

Harmison turned to Flintoff, with whom he had begun to forge a bond, in asking to return home early and the management agreed. Abrahams recalls that Harmison had not been expected to play a significant part in the tour because of his back injury. For Gifford, however, who was to hear of his young charge's difficulties with some trepidation, the problem was probably as much mental as physical.

"Yes, it was just being away," he says. "A kid from a pit village, he's gone to school, had a beer at the working men's club with his dad at a fairly young age. That was his life. He was taken away from all that and he found it very difficult to mix, and he was put in an environment where he thought: 'Christ, I'm not sure I can do this!' His reaction was to get back home."

For Steve Williams, Pakistan came too early for Harmison. He did not know anybody except for fellow Durham player John Graham. "I've never really asked him about it but it was a tough time for him." says Williams. "I think he just got a bit of a culture shock. The environment he comes from, the way we are – a very close-knit community. He's a quiet lad really. He was quite shy then. He just liked his close friends."

On his return, Harmison retreated into his shell. In later years, however, he would discuss the experience with engaging frankness. "That scarred me for life," he said. "I was a kid from the north-east suddenly sent to another country with another culture, another way of life, and I couldn't cope. I was just out of school and had never been away before. That's when my great friendship with Freddie Flintoff began. He's my best mate in the England team. I love him. All of a sudden I found I was in no state to continue playing and I went to see Freddie who was our captain. I knocked on his door and poured my heart out. He asked me to give it a week, then if I couldn't hack it, he would get me on the next plane home. I went back a week later and told him nothing had changed. Two days later, I was gone. He understood and helped me an awful lot."

His early return was not the perfect start to an England career. Indeed, had it not been for his massive potential, it could have cost him dearly. As it was, there was plenty of sympathy, even from his greatest champion before the tour. "The other selectors thought I was mad when I said he should go and even more mad when he came home," remembers Arnold. "We didn't know what he was like, with his homesickness, it was all out of the blue. I have never known it like that before, although I wasn't the greatest tourist myself when I was with England. The longer a trip went on, if you weren't having a great time, the more you wished you were home. When it was thrust upon him, it was at very short notice. He had only just started playing a few months before."

Wisden would later declare the seven-week tour of Pakistan a resounding success, adding: "Under the mature captaincy of Andrew Flintoff, a squad of emerging cricketers played confident, aggressive cricket, made friends and showed mental toughness." England had won both the unofficial Test series and the one-dayers, with the touring side's new-ball attack separating the sides. There was a short report highlighting noteworthy successes, detailed scorecards from the big games and results from the others. In all of this, Harmison's name did not feature once.

Harmison went home to his beloved Northumberland and vanished off the face of the earth – or so it must have seemed to those outside his close circle of family and friends. He had arrived on the cricket scene in a magical puff of smoke and departed in similar fashion. In effect, he turned his injured back on the game and, licking his wounds, reconsidered what to do for the rest of his life.

The chance of playing cricket for a living came with a hefty price tag attached. The temptation for someone so rooted must have been to follow his father's example and to restrict his sporting endeavours to the weekend, while earning a living in a more prosaic way. There would always be his days off, when he could go and cheer on Alan Shearer.

When Durham's squad assembled for the new season, their one-time promising pace bowler was nowhere to be seen. He was far from forgotten, however. Cook had been kept in the picture by the England Under-19 management. X-rays had been carried out on Harmison's back but Cook knew the injury – "it was nothing major, just one of those problems associated with a growing body" – was a side issue. Harmison's head was what really mattered. Had he retired, or just retired hurt?

"Yes, at that stage he was reconsidering the whole thing. He was genuinely not interested in playing cricket," says Cook. "I remember sitting down with the chief executive on quite a few occasions and saying: 'Look, this guy is a talent.' We had started to realise his character by that stage. We put forward a strategy, that we would leave him alone and take a step back. I take no credit for it at all. Simply, there were occasions in the middle of the winter where I would just drive up to see him in Ashington, to have a beer or whatever – just to talk, not necessarily about cricket.

"He said he didn't want to play cricket, he didn't want to be involved. I think it was an accumulation of things. I think the expectation was suddenly starting to get to him. He was in the Durham firsts, it was a little frightening, people were saying 'look out for him'. He hasn't always carried expectation that well, particularly in his early years.

"He loves playing, it's the peripheral stuff, the life of a cricketer, that he's not in love with – the practice regime, the commitment necessary. He loves to bowl, he loves to be on the pitch, but the time element of cricket was starting to hit home – a three-day match or a five-day match, a week away or whatever, coming down to nets every day. Add to that the

Pakistan experience, the expectation, the press, people saying he was the fastest young bowler for a long time. It just turned him off.

"I have always said that when someone signs a contract to play professionally their attitude to the game changes, subconsciously or consciously. It becomes a different entity altogether. Your whole attitude just changes. I'm not sure it has to. It loses the fun bit, which is tragic. You enjoy it in a different way, but as soon as you sign, the pressure starts.

"What we tried to do was to sell him Durham, not cricket, just the attractions of playing for Durham, and the convenience of it. We said he could get home every night and we could help in any way we could. There would be no pressure and he would do things at his own pace."

As a former Test bowler himself, Gifford, too, was determined not to let go without a fight. "We all knew he was too good to waste. We knew we had to get through this, he was too good for us to just wash our hands of and say he hadn't got the right attitude. There was too much potential there ever to do that.

"Geoff and I sat there thinking: 'This could be special. If we don't find a way to get him to realise that, it's all going to go to pot.' The idea was to see what would happen if we did not push, whether he would come back to us. I just hoped he might suddenly think: 'I'll give this cricket a go, I might be able to do something at that.' But yes, at one stage I did think we might lose him."

Cook, meanwhile, contacted Jimmy and Margaret Harmison to keep open a line of communication. "They are a very close family. I suppose their attitude was: 'We just want our Stephen to be happy.' I think Jimmy knew what he could be and I think he appreciated Durham's sensitivity. But he just wanted his son to be okay."

Ultimately, Cook and Gifford knew that the final decision

on Harmison's abortive career would be taken by the teenager himself. While Durham struggled throughout 1997 to escape the bottom of the County Championship table under new captain David Boon, press reports suggested S.J. Harmison, his back still creaking, was playing as a batsman for the Ashington Second XI. He would soon quietly reappear at Chester-le-Street, however, for a few net sessions.

"As I remember, to his credit, he made the first move and came back to us. It was always going to have to be up to Stephen to play," says Gifford. "You can help and guide and try to make sure it's an environment he's happy with, but that's all."

There was also a fleeting, single re-appearance for Durham's Second XI, bowling five overs for 27 runs without taking a wicket and making a pair. It was nothing too grand, but it was a start. As Cook says, "It was an open invitation, it wasn't dramatic, or overnight, at that stage he could have said: 'I'm not interested.' But I wouldn't have given up because I felt that, deep down, there was a love of playing cricket and it was a case of getting the right chemistry around that."

Perhaps, too, Harmison, with a little gentle nudging from his nearest and dearest, came to realise that the cricket pitch, whatever the drawbacks, offered a greener, more pleasant way of life than could ever be offered by the factory floor. As a school leaver, he had tried a mix of short-lived jobs, including labouring and night shifts at a foundry. After returning from Pakistan, he had worked with his father at an air conditioning unit plant at nearby Cramlington. Asked years later what he had been making while there, he had replied: "I haven't got a clue."

CHAPTER FOUR

AS MAD AS A CUT SNAKE

David Boon rolled into town in 1997 looking like a steely-eyed sheriff intent on cleaning up the place. All that was missing was two six-shooters, a star and a Stetson. Durham County Cricket Club, despite its grand designs, had yet to taste real success during five years of first-class existence. It was in danger, indeed, of turning into a curiosity – a first-class venue with a second-class team.

Boon, though, gazing out from behind his bristling, walrus moustache, had a reputation for Tasmanian toughness. He was a man's man who worked hard and played hard. Once, so the story goes and presumably as part of a personalised fitness regime, he had downed 52 cans of lager on the flight from Australia to England. The barrel-chested right-handed batsman had never been in the business of losing. He played in four Ashes-winning sides with the likes of Mark Taylor, Allan Border, Waugh, Warne and McGrath. He had hit the winning Ashes runs in 1989, which began Australia's unprecedented and unbroken streak of eight successive series victories. He had also been man of the match in the 1987 World Cup final, scoring 75 against England. He had carved out a reputation as a tenacious competitor who made the most of what talent he had. The sort of man, indeed, who you might ask to bat for your life.

When he arrived in the north-east he was already 37. He had played the last of his 107 Tests a year before. Durham would be his last challenge and he was keen to make a difference. He agreed to give it two years. Boon could not have come at a more important time. The team had suffered their worst season yet in 1996. They had failed to win a single game in the County Championship, claiming a third wooden spoon in five years. They had fared almost as badly in the one-day competitions, managing a single Sunday League success. Without Simon Brown's contribution – the left-arm quick was among the leading wicket-takers of the season, with 79 first-class victims – things would have looked bleaker still. The side's failings had cost Mike Roseberry his job as captain the previous August, leaving Boon to pick up the shards.

"We had had a terrible season, I think we'd won just one game in all," says Cook. "Morale in the team was low, individuals weren't producing as well as they could have done. We felt we had to change the captaincy and Mike agreed at the time it would be beneficial. I felt we needed a charismatic guy and we tried to get Dean Jones back but he had committed himself to Derbyshire. David Boon was perfect for us. It was the end on his Test career, so he was going to be fully available over an extended period. He showed some interest and we flew out to Tasmania and got him to sign as soon as possible.

"The idea was for him to use his own methods, but we wanted him to bring an element of competitiveness. We had forgotten how to compete. Through losing games, our young lads had lost that nous, that confidence to win games. He fitted the bill perfectly."

Boon was not surprised by what he saw. "In essence they were cruising," he says of the squad he inherited. "They were happy to be part of first-class cricket but there were certain things we had to do, and do quite quickly, and that was to learn how to win and to be positive and to really enjoy cricket."

He was astute enough, however, to realise that blazing away from the hip was not the best way forward, especially with the younger players.

"When I arrived there was relationship building and there was teaching the guys. We set up systems, we gave responsibility to players, teaching them to be honest with themselves rather than making up excuses. And we started developing a few young cricketers," he recalls.

There was to be no immediate, dramatic turnaround. Durham edged up one place in both County Championship and Sunday League in 1997. But there were two Championship victories, while Boon was delighted with "the improvement in commitment and attitude", adding: "All the counties we played against said there had been a vast change."

Towards the end of the season, Boon was asked to run the rule over a quick bowler, a young, quiet lad who Durham had been monitoring for the previous 12 months.

"I can remember our Stevie had had some time off from the game," says Boon. "He didn't play in my first year. It all went pear-shaped after his England Under-19 trip to Pakistan, but he came down the second year that I was there.

"The guys got him in for a bowl and I went along to watch. He was on his own, it wasn't a pre-season net. They didn't even let him bowl at anyone. They were just trying to get him back, under relaxed circumstances, without anyone around. I stood a little away at the start, then quickly moved to have a closer look.

"Basically I watched about three balls and went: 'Oh Jesus!' I just went to him and said: 'That's enough for me. Can you get yourself fit to play?' And that was it.

"He was tall, he had pace and I think that pace has grown as he has got stronger and matured. He was a bit gangly. He reminded me of some of the West Indians – big guys who run in with long levers and long arms. He was a bit wayward, but that didn't bother me. For us to have someone like him at Durham, hopefully to put the wind up a few people, would be a fantastic asset. It went from there."

Cook remembers the event as undramatic in the extreme. "Boony was fairly phlegmatic about anything, he never showed any emotion. Perhaps there was a wry smile, but that would have been it. David operated in his own style. There were no great histrionics. He worked with what he had got. He didn't say: 'I need this and this.' We had the responsibility to find the cricketers and he would captain them.

"I know Stephen bowled at Boony in the nets pretty early and knocked his stumps out a few times. I remember watching that. It's that sort of thing that makes an impression on Boon. After that, David played a great part in getting him on board."

Immediately after the net, Boon had cornered Cook and Gifford, seeking more information. Who was he? What had he done before and where had he been since? What was his background? What was he like? He quickly realised that Harmison would need time, and would have to be handled with care.

"He had gone into the England Under-19 set-up raw. I don't know what processes there were in those days for young guys or whether he knew what was involved, where he was going to go, and what was going to happen to him. But you could just see in his character that it wouldn't have sat that well with him in the beginning.

"Coming from a working-class area, north of the Tyne, it would have been a whole new world. Might he have quit after Pakistan? Look mate, I think it was definitely on the cards."

One was a batsman, one a bowler; one short and stocky, the other gangly; one a grizzled veteran, the other a fresh-faced novice. Standing side by side, Boon and Harmison looked almost comic together. But the pair quickly formed an unlikely bond.

"We became good mates," says Boon. "He's not a great talker on the phone but whenever our paths cross, time is made to catch up. It probably sounds funny coming from an Australian but I have been following his performances very closely. I've watched his progress and I feel very proud, I suppose, to have been a part of those couple of developmental years and his return to cricket."

For Gifford, Boon was to prove a huge and invaluable influence on many of Durham's youngsters, but he has particular praise for his handling of the young bowler.

"Boony was a hard taskmaster but he realised the talent Harmy had, and was understanding in where he came from, what the lad was like and what was needed. It wasn't a case of saying he had to fit in with everybody else, he knew there was something special in this boy and we had to find a way in bringing it out.

"It might mean bending the rules, of saying you've got to play in that game but you can go home after that. That was the way we found of working. Boony was brilliant."

The key, according to the Australian, was to use more carrot than stick. He accepts he demanded high standards but stresses there is more to him than his tough-as-teak public image.

"I wouldn't say he was petrified of me," he says, recalling that first meeting. "There's a lot of difference between blokes on and off the field. You don't compromise out there but I'm a great believer that cricket is a lot of fun. You have to enjoy it, and you have got to learn.

"My on-field persona didn't change at all but off the field I'm probably a fraction different, even if a lot of people don't realise that. Look, everybody has a compassionate side.

"Our major job, from my perspective, was to get him up

and enjoying cricket, to help him learn what it was all about. We had to get him out of that comfort zone, the north-east of England, and move forward because to me he was just a stand-out, someone who could be developed into the bowler that he is now and the bowler he could be in the future – one of England's best.

"It was just a case of him maturing and getting used to travelling. I think he has become a bit more comfortable with it now but in those days, even within England, he didn't like moving away from home.

"All I did was treat the guy as normally as possible, making sure he was included in everything and that he was happy. We had to get him into an environment and a thought process which meant he really wanted to play cricket, and really wanted to do well. It was just a bit of man management, really. He developed quite quickly, and the real credit for what he has achieved goes to him.

"I think the key to his success, for Durham and England, is the belief that people have confidence in him. Even if you have a gut feeling that someone can play, it is not often that they will succeed straight away. You have to give them time – time to develop and to get used to the first-class game, time to get used to Test cricket.

"I think that was the case with Harmy. In Test cricket England, for the first time for a while, gave someone an opportunity to settle in. They kept with him even though he was bowling short because they saw a talent. It can take one little performance, one shot as a batsman or one ball as a bowler, and all of a sudden it all clicks."

Durham enjoyed their most successful year to date in 1998, finishing 14th in the 18-team table. In early June, they had been as high as second before their form tailed off. Boon, caught up in the excitement, agreed to extend his contract for a third season.

"I think the stand-out thing Steve learnt from those years is that although pace means a fair bit, it is not the only thing that matters in a bowler. I was very pleased that, after I left, he pulled things back a bit – he got control, he got line and length – then he gradually moved up the pace once he got confident with that.

"It was fantastic for me too, taking on a young guy on a learning process. I feel proud of having been part of his career – I think he is fantastic."

Not that it was all that easy for the Australian. If Harmison felt out of place in Pakistan, then Boon had as much reason to feel foreign in the football-mad north-east when he first arrived. For a start, there was the accent.

"To me he was… ah mate, he was a Geordie. As mad as a cut snake.

"He's a bloody good kid, he listened, he learned, he thought, he had fire in his belly when he got a bit more confident. When he got excited during matches, though, I had to get the interpreter out. I had no idea what he was carrying on about. Colly [Paul Collingwood] used to field at first slip and I asked him what he had said and he'd let me know.

"A lot of the time it was basically along the lines of: 'Captain, I want to kill this bloke, and if you take me off I'll kill you.' When I had him calm we did speak in English, but outside of that he lapsed back into Geordie. No wonder he doesn't sledge batsmen. Of course, if you bowl like him, you don't have to, but with Harmy it would be a waste of time. Nobody can understand what he's saying anyway.

"He did a good job for the team in 1998 and 1999. My son Jack loved him. He was about seven or eight at the time but he and Harmy got on really well. Jack still talks about him.

"Harmy is not pretentious and he doesn't take anything for granted. He's straight down the line, no frills or wrapping paper or anything like that. What you see is what you get."

Football was another new language for the Tasmanian.

"Does he like football? Mate, he's a nutter. All the English are nutters. It's a bloody religion. I had a split dressing room between Sunderland and Newcastle. Colly's Sunderland, Harmy's Newcastle and they'd carry on at each other all the time."

Boon in particular remembers a local soccer derby between the sides, which tested his patience to the limit. "I told them one night I didn't want them to go to St James' Park. I told them I probably wasn't in a position to stop them but, if they insisted they had to go, I did not want anyone wearing team colours. I found out the next morning that three of my boys wore Sunderland colours and had to run away after the game. I wasn't too happy about it.

"Harmy loved all that, though. It's a side that most people don't see. He stirred the dressing room up like you wouldn't believe when Sunderland got relegated. He stirred the living daylights out of them.

"There I was, trying to prepare the team on the morning of a first-class match and he was dancing about the dressing room and I had five grown men sitting there in tears. It was something I just couldn't fathom. I went to St James' Park a few times but I never really got it."

What he did get, however, was Harmison's mental make-up.

Many have equated the Englishman's shyness and apparent reluctance to travel as a weakness. Boon disagrees and invites such commentators to enter a cricket net with Harmison to settle the issue.

"It was a funny thing, he was not shy when he felt comfortable. When he didn't feel comfortable he was really shy and withdrawn. But he's a credit to himself, from where he's come from and what he has had to learn and where he has had to go. I would totally disagree with anybody who says he is weak.

"It was just a learning curve. If you face Harmison at the other end of the nets or in a cricket match, you know there is something coming at you and you know it's a battle. He is showing that now he's settled in international cricket.

"How good can he get? That's like asking how long is a piece of string. Anyone can be as good as they want to be if they put the work in, and that target is probably unlimited. He's young enough. I think he could be England's premier fast bowler for quite some time to come.

"I just hope he does not get too many wickets against Australia. I'd have mixed feelings if he does well against Australia. He can do well, as long as Australia still win."

The affection between the two men is mutual. Under the section 'Sportsmen particularly admired' in the *Cricketers' Who's Who,* Harmison included three names: Alan Shearer, David Boon and Courtney Walsh.

Harmison has always worshipped the Newcastle striker as a footballing god. Betting on him scoring the first goal for Newcastle every match, week in, week out, is almost a religion to him. Walsh, the West Indian fast bowler, was also revered as a cricketing extra-terrestrial. Boon, in contrast, provided a very human, personal influence.

Pre-season county cricket press days rarely offer much to journalists other than chilblains and banalities. Nobody has much to say and it is usually too cold to talk anyway. Thus it was when Durham unveiled their squad at Chester-le-Street in April 1998. It is doubtful, indeed, whether many of the local hacks even noticed the tall, spotty, slim newcomer with the questionable haircut, tucked away on the end of the back row of the squad picture. Harmison looked like a slightly bemused afterthought as he stood to attention next to the Second XI scorer. Those who did remember the name from two years previously might have questioned the wisdom of the recruitment but Boon knew better and countered bluntly:

"He is being strongly considered for a full-time contract. I think he can bowl."

The immediate omens, however, were not good. Harmison's away debut for Durham, one-and-a-half years after his wretched first home appearance, looked like a recipe for disaster. As in 1996, he was propelled into the side by adverse circumstances. Brown, the mainstay of the attack throughout Durham's formative years, broke down at the start of the season with a cruciate ligament injury that would require surgery. Harmison was thus selected to play against Brian Lara's Warwickshire at Edgbaston.

To this day, the words Lara, Warwickshire and Edgbaston are enough to bring Durham players and fans out in a cold sweat. Only four years previously the West Indies batsman, fresh from scoring a then-Test world record 375 against England in Antigua, had padded up and taken guard against Durham on the same ground. After a scratchy start Lara had got to 18, only to snick a simple chance behind. The unfortunate Chris Scott dropped it. "I suppose he'll get another century now," the wicket-keeper reportedly mumbled. Lara, however, did not score one hundred but five, one on top of the other, in achieving a first-class world-record score of 501.

Lara was returning in 1998 as Warwickshire captain. They were the County Championship favourites, while Durham, booming off the field but struggling on it, were 500-1 outsiders. It was a massacre waiting to happen and Harmison must have been experiencing flashbacks of his West Indian trauma from 1996 as he changed into his whites.

He was not the only one feeling some trepidation. Martin Speight, Durham's wicket-keeper – who came from Brighton and, like Boon, could barely understand a word that Harmison uttered during those early days – was constantly being reminded of Scott's butter-fingered misfortune. "There was a lot of talk about Lara coming back and I was getting quizzed a lot of the time as the wicket-keeper. Everyone remembered that drop," he says.

Boon had to decide before the game whether to go with Harmison or the more dependable Alan Walker. "He opted for Harmy, even though he'd barely seen him bowl more than once in the nets," recalls Speight. The match had barely begun, however, when a larger-than-average problem arose. "As I remember, Kenny Palmer was umpiring and said something about it. Harmy had no decent boots. His shoes were falling apart. The game had already started and Boony had to sort him out with a new pair."

For Speight, things began almost perfectly. "Fortunately, Lara nicked one behind to me on nought off John Wood and I didn't drop it. Actually I caught him in both innings, both times off Wood." Harmison, however, his long curtains of hair flopping down over his eyes and his nerves jangling, opened with a succession of long hops and full tosses. But, swinging the ball into the left handers, he came back to take two wickets. In the second innings he did even better, sending front-line batsmen Nick Knight and David Hemp's stumps cartwheeling on his way to overall figures of five for 150 in a drawn match. "He used to swing it quite a bit then. He wasn't as quick but it was quick enough," says Speight. "In the end, he bowled really well. I remember Gifford saying Durham would be lucky to keep hold of him because Warwickshire would have realised he had some serious potential."

There was a West Indian flavour to Harmison's first home match of the season as well. Again he found himself playing against an all-time West Indian great, and one with whom he would later be compared. Courtney Walsh took six wickets for 42 in the second innings to ensure a Gloucestershire success, but Harmison managed five for 70 himself (figures he would not better that year) in the first innings and three for 32 in the second. He even helped save the follow-on batting at number 11 by keeping Walsh out in the first innings.

At other times, he was less impressive. "He's like a sports car," says Speight. "If it's fine-tuned, it's brilliant. If it's slightly off, it's rubbish, or pretty close to it."

His most noteworthy success, however, was to come at Lord's in June. Again he would find himself pitted against a world-class opponent and again he would leave a mark, or, in this case, several black-and-blue marks.

Australia's Justin Langer was a batsman of proven pedigree. Middlesex, with Mike Gatting also in their top order, had never lost to Durham. Few, if any of them, would have heard of Harmison. Langer certainly had not. He and the Middlesex top-order, however, were soon being peppered with a barrage of fast, sharply rearing deliveries. Langer, skipping about like a kangaroo, survived the onslaught only to fall to Melvyn Betts at the other end in both innings.

"He bowled really well there," Gifford recalls. "You could tell Langer was thinking: 'Bloody hell, where's this kid come from?' When you watched him bowl at someone like that and trouble him, you thought: 'Christ he's giving him a bit of a working-over!' And you thought if he could do it to a batsman of his class, and a tough boy and all, then there had to be something different about him."

For Boon, the Lord's game was the highlight of the season. "I think the stand-out game was him bowling at Langer," he recalls. "He had him jumping all over the shop and hitting him a couple of times. That was the day I thought: 'This kid's coming of age.'

"Langer came straight over and said: 'Where have you got him from? He's just awesome. He's seriously quick.' He said it was the quickest bowling he had faced that year in any style of cricket. Steve had his moments that season. He hurried a lot of players up. At times he was the enforcer, a bit like Merv Hughes was for Australia, one of those blokes who would get everyone on the back foot and often the guys at the other end would reap the rewards of what he was doing."

Harmison took four for 88 in the first innings and three for 57 in the second against Middlesex, sharing 16 wickets with Betts. The two, at the time, were the top wicket-takers in the championship. They even teamed up to produce a fairytale finish after Durham had been set 240 to win. They were the last pair at the crease, and nine were still needed off two overs. Betts launched Phil Tufnell's left-arm spin into the stands for a six, then two tail-enders scampered three more to seal victory.

Looking back, those performances seem more extraordinary still when Harmison's difficulties with leaving home are taken into account. Gifford remembers that he would get homesick at away games and every effort was made to get him back to Ashington as soon as was feasible. Those interpreting that hankering as a character flaw, though, would have been confused by a natural confidence that quickly emerged as he began to feel more comfortable within the team.

"A lot of people get the wrong impression," says Cook. "He is quite shy in some respects. But he very much knows his own mind and has always known it, particularly on sporting matters. He'll make his point quite forcefully when the need arises. He was very much at the centre of activity and a contributor to everything that went on."

Speight concurs. "He does have a confidence, a slightly harsh confidence, about him that comes from his background. If you meet him socially, he's very confident. He's had to be, growing up in Ashington. It's a tough place. The north-east has become a lot easier than it was when I first moved up there around ten years ago. It has softened a lot, but it is still a hard place to grow up, make no mistake about it. It is very parochial."

Bizarrely, Harmison's lack of cricket culture seemed to help in some ways. "He wouldn't have known anybody he was playing against when he started," says Speight. "He was like Ed Giddins. I remember when Ed started, he ran up and got Viv Richards out. He didn't know who Richards was, so he wasn't fazed.

"I remember during the Scarborough festival, we were all out with the Yorkshire lads in a night club. Darren Gough at the time was England's number one – character, bowler and cricketer. He had a cigarette behind his ear, like a workman's pencil, and he was talking to Harmy. Whether they could understand each other, I'm not sure. Anyway, that cigarette started to annoy Steve. He was only a young kid but he picked it out from behind Gough's ear, and said: 'If you are going to smoke it, get on with it or else get rid of it.' Then he threw it on the floor and stamped on it."

Gifford, meanwhile, was aware of another apparently confusing contradiction in the county's new strike bowler – a player totally committed on the pitch but less so off it.

"When he was there and bowling, he was super. But his first love was football. If you had given the kid the choice then of signing professional terms with Durham County Cricket Club or playing for Newcastle United, we wouldn't have been in the hunt – no chance," says Gifford. "From where he came from, he and all his mates wouldn't have been dreaming about cricket. It would be bloody football.

"In terms of seriously taking cricket up as a career, he was going through the motions. But when he went out and played he was quite serious, he was not a sulky boy who would pack it in if things did not go right. You never had any of that. But you wondered whether it was really what he wanted to do."

Perhaps inevitably, the 1998 season would tail off for both Durham and their young quicks as fatigue and injuries took their toll. Harmison, still filling out physically, began to suffer from shin splints, a common phenomenon among young fast bowlers. When the England Under-19 selectors picked him to make his debut in the first of three 'Tests' against a visiting Pakistan in August, he pulled out with a calf problem, having already bowled more than 400 overs that campaign.

Durham's excellent start to the season, though, paved the way for their highest position in the Championship to date. Fourteenth place left Boon wondering what might have been. That question was exciting enough to convince him to delay his retirement and return for one more season.

There was to be no rest at the end of the season for Harmison, however, just further recognition. While Flintoff was chosen overwhelmingly as the Cricket Writers' Young Player of the Year, the Durham bowler was named a runner-up with Middlesex batsman Owais Shah.

His "remarkable emergence", as *Wisden* put it – he took 51 first-class wickets at 30.29 apiece – also led to selection for England A's tour of Zimbabwe and South Africa after a single full season. His touring problems in 1996-7 had been consigned to history.

"If anyone had told me at the start of this season I would be going on an England A tour, I would have laughed in their face," Harmison responded in an interview with Tim Wellock of the *Northern Echo*. "Last year there were times I thought I would never play for Durham again. Going on the A tour will not be as big a step as it was going from Ashington to Parkistan with England under-19s."

He was right. This time he would come through the experience unscathed, even if there were few fireworks on the pitch. He took seven wickets in three matches, at an average of 38.85 – making him statistically the worst of the front-line bowlers by a margin – but he was selected for the second 'Test' against Zimbabwe, taking two wickets in the first innings, including that of future Test player Stuart Carlisle. It was his potential, however, which again made him stand out. *Wisden*'s report remarked: "The success of England A tours is not supposed to be judged by results. The aim is to produce players who can progress to the full England side. Of the quick bowlers, Steve Harmison appeared best equipped to step up. He struggled at the outset but, as the tour progressed, gained control without losing pace, and troubled good batsmen with channelled aggression. He often had third man posted ten yards in from the boundary to become an attacking fielder looking for the top edge."

The other plus was that Harmison was beginning to team up with players who, for varying reasons, would later play important roles in his future career, including Flintoff, Robert Key and Michael Vaughan.

CHAPTER FIVE

GROWING PAINS

Harmison's first full season had coincided with Durham's most successful County Championship campaign. In his second – and Boon's last of an illustrious career – things got better still.

Harmison, now promoted to the front row of the team photograph, would win his county cap in 1999, top the side's wicket-taking table with a 64 first-class victims at 27.73 runs apiece, and help Durham to their best finish in their short history. He even found time to get married (to his childhood sweetheart, Hayley), as well as celebrating the birth of his first daughter. England's selectors, with former Durham captain David Graveney at their head, kept their ears to the ground and their binoculars pointing north.

Durham was not the place to be, however, on the opening day of the season. The first newspaper photographs of Harmison did not involve exploding stumps, just exploding snowballs, as Chester-le-Street disappeared under an inch of snow on the first morning of the club's opening match against Worcestershire.

Harmison took time to warm up. Towards the end of April, struggling for rhythm, he had managed just one wicket in the defeat against Hampshire. Against Kent and Yorkshire in May, he did not manage to disturb a single batsman and Durham were bottom of the table. "He bowled absolute rubbish for a lot of the time in those days, before he got it together," Micky Stewart recalls. In June, to compound matters, the team travelled to Amstelveen and contrived to lose to Holland, captained by former Somerset all rounder Roland Lefebvre, in the NatWest Trophy.

On top of that, there would be the injury problems which would persist for several years. He may not have been the keenest of trainers, but his growing pains did not help him. "The biggest problem with Harmy early on was that he had shin splints all the time," recalls Speight. "So he never had time to practise in the nets. If he bowled six or seven balls, you would be lucky. He might have a little jog through in the middle but every single break in play you'd see him with bags of ice on his shins. He was limited in what he could do."

Harmison, however, gradually roused himself from his hibernation as the sun broke through. His captain opted to reserve him for Championship matches rather than one-day thrashes, although that did not stop Boon working him hard – some thought too hard – and long, as the team came to rely on his strike bowling.

There were five Harmison wickets in the draw against Somerset and seven against Northamptonshire, including that of last man and former England strike bowler Devon Malcolm, to secure Durham's first Championship win for 12 months.

Speight, who has since forged a career as an artist, recalls that particular game with a smile and a wince. "Harmy used to like his 'pop' back then," he says. "It began raining heavily on the third evening and Harmy took a gamble on there being no play on the last day and went out for a drink. You don't like to admit that it goes on but certain people do risk it. Wantage Road, though, dries out very quickly. When we got to the ground it was underwater and he had fallen asleep in the changing room. But suddenly it was 3 pm and we were starting. If play had begun at 11 o'clock, he wouldn't have been able to stand, let alone bowl."

Durham's 12th man was already on the field after Boon's problems with a broken left hand. At tea, a draw looked likely. Harmison, nursing his sore head, had managed nothing of note. "But then Harmy came back and bowled with real fire for almost 20 overs non-stop. I was standing miles back. The worst thing about keeping to him is that, when he gets the ball past the bat, it wobbles all over the place. He got one through about head height and I tried to reverse-cup it, with my fingers pointing up. I went a little early and the ball floated up and hit me right on the end of my middle left finger. Two balls later I took my glove off to have a look. The first joint of the finger was doubled backwards, it was dislocated and broken straight down the joint. But we had no one else to come on, so the physio put the finger back in, strapped it up and I carried on.

"We ended up winning the game and Harmy got the last three or four wickets. We had about eight slips for him. I missed the next game but the following week Boony said: 'I don't care if it's broken, I need you to play.' That was the Australian way. By all accounts Ian Healey (Australia's wicket-keeper) played with his fingers all over the oche. You just got on and did it. Even today, when I go out to defrost the car on cold days, I have about four fingers which go white."

Durham were crushed by Surrey at The Oval at the start of July but Harmison, his snap back, took the second five-wicket haul of his career in the first innings, accounting for both Hollioake brothers.

Adam, who also succumbed to Harmison in the second innings, was impressed. "I knew he was something different, a bit of a freak. You don't get many blokes as big as him whanging it down at 90mph. They don't fall out of trees," he says. "You always say about people like that, if they get it right, then they will be very special. People like Flintoff and Harmison, they come along once in a blue moon."

Nottinghamshire were the next side to travel to the north-east and lose, before Harmison helped force Derbyshire into submission. At its most brutal, cricket can be a terrifying game, especially for batsmen repeatedly asked to fend off projectiles travelling towards their throats faster than third-lane motorway traffic. That day, the men of Derby failed to find the courage to meet the challenge – one was struck on the helmet and several others took blows to hands and body – and were blown away for 130 in their second innings. They headed home after losing inside two days.

On the final day of the season, and in a perfect send-off for Boon, Durham drew with Leicestershire, earning themselves eighth place in the table and ensuring a spot in the First Division when the Championship was divided the following year.

In truth, Harmison had not produced too many headline-grabbing performances during the season – he was still trading on potential and exciting pace rather than on solid achievements – but his stock was rising, just at a time when England were beginning to talk of finding fresh bowling blood. And not just any old medium-paced plasma, either. The search would soon be on for something rather more singular.

David Lloyd, the England coach, had already moaned about the dearth of match-winning bowlers being created by the County Championship. There was the usual production line of trundlers able to exploit English green-tops in chilly, overcast conditions, but when would England discover a bowler of genuine, searing pace or a spinner of prodigious turn?

After a wretched 1999 World Cup, however, Lloyd was gone. England, barracked by their own fans, had just lost to New Zealand at home and found themselves at the bottom of the world Test rankings.

Former Zimbabwe batsman Duncan Fletcher took over, teaming up with new captain Nasser Hussain. Their first job would be to bind English wounds. If spectacular players were not immediately available, then the priority would be to create a bloody-minded, backs-to-the-wall team that would at least be stubbornly determined to avoid defeat. It would not be pretty but it would help rebuild self-respect.

Fletcher, who appears in public as a dour man with a short ration of smiles, and Hussain, a player whose reputation was built as much on determination as natural talent, would personify their team. The search for the spectacular would have to wait.

At least the selectors were talking about starting with a blank sheet of paper, even if they were not ready to gamble on untested youth. A debate soon followed over which young players might emerge to speed up the team's recovery. Yorkshire's Vaughan, with three A tours behind him, the last as captain, and Vikram Solanki of Worcestershire, a man of Asian deftness, topped the list. Key, from Kent, was frequently mentioned in dispatches. Flintoff of Lancashire and Ben Hollioake of Surrey were being groomed as exciting all-rounders. Among the bowlers, the Yorkshireman Matthew Hoggard was a contender. So was Harmison.

But while each had their champions – and Ian Botham would become increasingly vocal in Harmison's cause – each also had detractors. Harmison's difficulties on his ill-fated Under-19 tour would be unearthed and recycled by more than one national newspaper. The implication was that, desperate though England might be for new cricketing heroes, this model was perhaps not one to be encouraged. In August 1999, *The Guardian* ran the rule over a string of young players. "All it required was for Justin Langer, Middlesex's Australian batsman, to call Harmison 'seriously fast' and the media took interest," it said. "Harmison was also seriously fast on the England Under-19 tour to Pakistan three years ago, leaving it in a hurry because of homesickness. Skinny bowler of some promise, assisted by Durham's seamer-friendly pitches." It was not a resounding endorsement.

England, though, appeared to have faith and selected him for the A tour of Bangladesh and New Zealand under captain Mark Alleyne and tour manager Mike Gatting. They even nominated him as injury cover for the full tour to South Africa. But that winter Harmison went nowhere.

After playing in Durham's final county game against Leicestershire in mid-September Harmison was chosen to spend a few team-building days with the A squad in the Lake District. Soon after, he pulled out of the two-month trip at the very last minute with a knee problem.

Durham said it had been a marginal decision, prompted by caution after Harmison's Herculean efforts in the County Championship, when he had bowled just short of 600 overs – almost 100 more than any of his team-mates. England, the club said, had simply decided against the risk of taking him on tour.

Soon, rumours began to circulate. Nothing appeared in the press but it would be recounted in county dressing rooms that Harmison had simply wanted to stay at home. The most colourful rumour suggested he had turned back at the airport check-in. It is tempting to speculate that more than one factor was involved, as in 1996-7. To complicate matters, this time he had a young family.

Cook says the tale of the airport check-in was not far off the mark.

"It's nearly true. He certainly did withdraw late. He rang me as he was about to leave for the airport. He was flying from Newcastle and joining up with the rest of the team at Gatwick or somewhere. It was a Friday evening, and he telephoned and said: 'I can't go.' He had had the injury, and he legitimately didn't feel as though he was fit enough to go on the tour. So I told him he had to do the contacting and then, on the Saturday morning, I met him with the chief executive and we talked things over and told him to forget about it.

"There are two phases to that thing. You have to deal with the lad immediately, because he was very, very upset. He felt as though he was letting everybody down, himself included, and his family and England.

"He knew his reputation. He didn't want to make that worse but he genuinely felt he couldn't go on tour. We had to appease him and make him feel we supported that decision. Once we got over that, we had to produce a plan for him to work through the remainder of the winter."

It was as delicate a time for Harmison and Durham as it had been two years before after his return from Pakistan. "He had got in the first team and settled with Boony and his mates, and that was fine," says Gifford. "But his ability was always going to take him through the Under-19s and A teams and the whole process would start again. He would be pushed into an area with few friends and he must have thought: 'I've got to suffer this all over again.' He found that very difficult."

At one stage, Durham County Cricket Club chairman Bill Midgley even considered approaching Newcastle United manager Bobby Robson, who had had such an influence on Paul Gascoigne and whom Harmison revered, to see if he might talk to the young bowler in an attempt to alleviate his homesickness problem.

Cook's immediate concern, however, was to prevent Harmison giving up altogether. "We had to make sure he was not going to be lost to cricket," he says. "Yes, it was a worry then as well. It was continuous, really. Our focus was Stephen, not his reputation."

Despite his winter setback Harmison, and indeed Durham, began the new millennium well placed to push on to greater things. After a good 1998 and an excellent 1999, both player and club now needed to step things up. Durham was ready to stage an international match for the first time and this was also the year, so suggested the perfect script, that Harmison would play for England.

He had avoided the common pitfall of failing to capitalise after an impressive debut season. In 2000, however, he had to begin a campaign burdened for the first time by expectation. He had been A.N. Other at the start of his first season and not much more than an exciting prospect for his second, but he was now an automatic choice with growing responsibilities. The national selectors were also taking an interest. Indeed, they had been interested from the very start.

"I can't exactly remember when I saw him first, but it would have been in 1998," says Graveney, England's head of selectors. "He just reminded me of the way Courtney Walsh bowls. He did it very easily.

"We (the selectors) are talent scouts in essence. We go around, watching games. We obviously can't be in every place on every single day. Every selector has a network of contacts and captains he consults. I tend to go to clubs and ask them not necessarily about their own players but about those of the sides they play against. I think you probably give a far more balanced view of an opponent, as opposed to one of your own players – it lends more credence. I'd talk to umpires as well. A lot of the guys these days have played the game. We go in all directions. Then, as the season goes on, we concentrate on certain individuals. Harmy would have been someone we would have watched.

"They always say the best players have time to play. Well, when Harmy bowls, the best players don't have that much time. That was the impression that was coming back from good players on the county scene."

Recognition was to come quickly. Harmison's season could not have started better. Durham, hosting champions Surrey in early May in their opening First Division encounter, must have been daunted, having lost to their opponents in 18 previous matches in all competitions since 1992. The Londoners marched in with a full international line-up, including Mark Butcher, Graham Thorpe and the Hollioake brothers among the batsmen and West Indian Ian Bishop, Martin Bicknell and Ian Salisbury fronting the bowling. Durham, in contrast, had Brown's one England test cap to boast of, while the comforting, ample presence of Boon had been replaced by fresh-faced Western Australian left-hander Simon Katich.

Three days later, however, the home team had won by 231 runs, having swept away their much-vaunted opponents for 104 and 85. Surrey do not lose by such margins, even on sporting pitches. It was a result certain to raise the eyebrows of England's selectors. The big headlines went to Brown and Neil Killeen, who exploited the damp, seaming conditions to take six wickets each, as well as to 17-year-old Nicky Peng, who missed out on a debut century by two runs. Harmison, though, produced enough steepling bounce and pace to make an impression, particularly on England left-hander Thorpe, who he dismissed cheaply in both innings. Harmison's second innings figures of 12-4 -19-2 also pointed to growing control.

Five wides in an over at a key stage of a Benson and Hedges Cup quarter-final defeat to Lancashire did much to reverse that impression – "Harmison's struggles degenerated into embarrassment," the *Northern Echo* reported – but his fine Championship form continued in the next game as he spread-eagled the stumps of John Crawley and Flintoff on the way to taking four for 74 against the same opponents.

Those performances were enough to propel him into

England's first Test squad of the summer. On the third day of the Championship game against Lancashire, Harmison and uncapped 21-year-old leg spinner Chris Schofield – awarded an England central contract after barely a season of first-class cricket – discovered they had both been selected in the 13 to take on Zimbabwe at Lord's the following week.

"There had been some talk in the papers about me," he told the *Northern Echo's* Tim Wellock. "But it was still a big surprise when I got the call. My bowling has never been timed, so I don't know exactly how fast I bowl. I hope to find out on Thursday.

"It would be great to get in the team and stay there for the series against the West Indies. Curtly Ambrose and Courtney Walsh are phenomenal and I would love to play against them and see them at close hand."

England would have to pick four specialist bowlers from a battery of five – Darren Gough, Andy Caddick, Giddins, Harmison and Schofield.

Gough and Caddick were automatic picks. The damp weather did not favour Schofield but his central contract suggested he would play. It came down, thus, to selecting either Harmison or Giddins. The former offered out-and-out pace, the latter a combination of swing and seam ideally suited for the conditions. Giddins was aged 28 to Harmison's 21, and hardly represented the future of English bowling, but swing and spin won out. Giddins and Schofield played and Harmison, deprived of the opportunity of making a low-key debut, was released. The same thing would happen a fortnight later in the Second Test.

At Lord's Zimbabwe, in their first appearance at cricket's headquarters, were destroyed by an innings and 209 runs inside three days. The selectors were able to boast that they had got things half right as Giddins took the man-of-the-match award. Feeding off a green pitch and murky cloud cover, he took five for 15 runs in seven overs in the first innings as the touring side were bowled out for 83. Giddins removed Andy Flower with his fourth ball and then ran through the middle-order. He added two more wickets in the second innings, when Gough and Caddick did the damage with four wickets apiece.

Schofield's selection was a less obvious success. Patently unsuited to the conditions, he spent most of the match looking on. England bowled 68.5 overs in all and the leg spinner was not afforded a single one of them. To cap a miserable debut, he was dismissed for a third-ball duck.

England, however, felt duty bound to retain the same side after their biggest Test victory for more than 25 years. Hussain remained cautious as he continued rebuilding his side's morale, arguing: "There are no easy games in Test cricket, especially for us. It might be easy for Australia to 'blood' a couple of lads but our first aim is just to win."

At Trent Bridge, the touring side made a fight of it and came away with a creditable draw, Murray Goodwin making a century. England only managed to take five wickets in a rain-affected encounter. Giddins got one but Schofield again had a poor time of it. After hitting an unorthodox if inventive 57, he bowled 18 overs for 73 runs without success. He was not selected again and, within a few years, could not even make the Lancashire side, eventually playing as a batsman who bowled a bit.

Giddins fared little better. The last of his four Tests came against West Indies in his next match and, after several county switches, he retired in 2003.

Harmison, meanwhile, returned to the Riverside. He had been given a peek into the England set-up and seen what was required. Not everyone, though, agreed with the way he had been handled.

"My big regret is that they didn't pick him to play

Zimbabwe at Lord's," says Steve Williams. "It showed how naive the selectors were, to pick horses for courses against such a poor team as Zimbabwe – picking Giddins, instead of blooding Steve, when we were playing the West Indies later that season. It would have given him the experience, even if he had not played all those games. It held him back two years.

"He was absolutely gutted. It still annoys me now. My son Greg went to the game with Steve's dad and his brother James. They travelled all the way down and came back the same night. They saw Hussain give the nod to Giddins on the first morning and then Stephen just walked away."

He walked, or rather hobbled, away again later that summer. Included in the first squad against the West Indies, he had to withdraw with his perennial shin problems. Had he been selected, he would have found himself playing against Walsh and Curtly Ambrose, two fast bowlers with whom Harmison would later be compared. By then, though, Harmison's form was on the wane and he was discarded for the rest of a glorious season as England recorded their first series success over the men from the Caribbean for 31 years.

Cook has no complaints over the way Harmison was handled by England coach Fletcher. "He believes you want seven or eight fast bowlers as a national core. He saw Harmison as one of those and he was going to get him involved in some shape or form. Stephen was still a young lad and had a lot of maturing in front of him. Fletcher wanted him to have every opportunity to mature in the England environment.

"They never really asked about his character, which was good. They didn't want him to take any baggage with him. He was bowling okay in 2000 – it was just a question of handling the new environment. So I think the softly-softly approach in getting him involved before the absolute exposure was just about right.

"He was finding out what was needed. He recognised it was the England environment where he wanted to be, and he was trying very hard. He was very impressed with people like Hussain and Gough, people who in different ways showed Stephen what it was to be professional, and what cricket at the highest level was about. I think he wanted to make sure that he was part of that."

There was a downside, however. The harder Harmison tried to impress, the fewer wickets he seemed to take and the worse he seemed to bowl. His shins a continual problem, his struggles would spill into the following season.

"My impression was that during his first two seasons he knew how to get people out," says Cook. "He knew his method. But the message from England was that they wanted fast and aggressive bowlers. That probably got into his subconscious and I think he tried to bowl a little faster and shorter than he had done before. It was a little bit frustrating for us that he wasn't performing as we knew he could. It wasn't through lack of effort. After that second season he wasn't a prolific wicket-taker. Those two years were transitional. But I could see an upward trend developing."

Graveney adds: "I could remember my period as captain with Gloucestershire when David Lawrence and Jack Russell were being touted for England in the press. It's very difficult for players who haven't played at international level when their names are always being mentioned in the papers. They tend to ask themselves; 'What more do I have to do?' Perhaps they then try a bit too hard to impress. It's very difficult. What can you say to a player? Is it five or ten more wickets and then you've done enough? All you can do is say: 'Look, you're in the mix and you just have to keep performing.'"

The year ended miserably as Durham slid down the table

and towards inevitable relegation into Division Two. Harmison could not buy a wicket, his bowling increasingly scatter-gun. *Wisden* thought him worthy of just a couple of sentences in reviewing the Durham campaign. "The biggest disappointment was Steve Harmison's increasing lack of control," it said. "After being included in the season's first three England squads, he suffered from sore shins, and his form on his return was awful."

Durham's County Championship campaign ended in a perfect mirror image of its start as the team travelled south to The Oval and lost by an innings and 68 runs. Harmison went for four an over as he took two for 105 and bowled seven wides, to the jeers of a small crowd, as Mark Butcher and Ian Ward both scored hundreds and put on 359 for Surrey's first wicket. Surrey marched on to the Championship and Durham descended dismally into the Second Division.

The *Northern Echo* commented that its favourite bowler "desperately needs a top coach to help him get a highly promising career back on track". Cook and Gifford were equally wary, even if they kept their thoughts private. "I used to speak a lot with Norman," Cook says. "We used to say he's either going to be the very best or he won't even be a county cricketer. It was the type of bowler he was. He wanted to be a fast, aggressive bowler. There was the trying to impress England and the injury frustrations, and that affected him psychologically. He looked like he was finding cricket tough."

Improbably, after taking a mere 26 first-class wickets, less than half his tally in 1999, at 31.61 runs apiece, Harmison was still selected for the England A tour of the Caribbean. Durham were not too sure of the wisdom of that decision, perhaps preferring to wrap their bowler in cotton wool for the winter. England, though, were still intent on taking a leap of faith with the young man from Ashington, whatever the immediate evidence. Two months of playing in the Caribbean and taking part in the Busta Cup would surely provide invaluable experience.

Exhausted, Harmison pulled out injured.

Erratic from first to last, Harmison slipped ever further out of England contention in 2001. England had a wretched summer. Hosting the gifted Pakistanis and the peerless Australians, the home team, ravaged by injuries to the likes of Hussain, Thorpe and Vaughan, suffered the bloodiest of noses, losing five Tests out of seven and all six games in the NatWest triangular one-day series.

The bowling attack was led by the experienced pairing of Gough and Caddick. The support bowling, however, was less impressive. Gough and Caddick shared 16 wickets for 207 runs in the first Test of the summer, a victory over Pakistan at Lord's, but left-arm seamer Ryan Sidebottom, the latest England experiment, failed to take his chance. Without a wicket, he was dropped after a single appearance, just as his father Arnie had been 15 years earlier.

For the rest of the summer the increasingly exasperated selectors supplemented the attack with all-rounders Craig White and Dominic Cork, quicks like Allan Mullally, Hoggard and the injury-jinxed Tudor, and the spinners Ashley Giles, Robert Croft and Phil Tufnell. They never settled on a trustworthy combination. The Ashes series, which ended in a 4-1 Australian mauling, culminated at The Oval with another new face in swing bowler Jimmy Ormond. Like Sidebottom, he failed to establish himself and was soon consigned to history.

During all this, Harmison was out of sight if not out of mind as he struggled with his game and his overworked body. It was an unsettling time at Chester-le-Street, Gifford having been replaced by Martyn Moxon as coach and with the Durham attack in transition.

The situation cried out for Harmison to step up as

Durham's chief wicket-taker but his successes were to be sporadic and his form untrustworthy as the club finished one from bottom of Division Two in the County Championship. His best performance came against the division champions, Sussex – a career-best six for 111 in July (after finishing the first day with one for 80). In a withering spell of fast bowling a month later at Hove, he claimed four of the first five Sussex wickets to fall as they were skittled for a season-low total of 117 on their way to a rare defeat.

Thirty-five wickets at just over 36 apiece, however, did not suggest much improvement. Nor did he contribute much to Durham's single achievement of the season as they won promotion to the first flight of the Norwich Union League. It was team-mate and friend Paul Collingwood who supplanted him in England's affections during the summer as the batting all-rounder earned the first of his one-day caps.

England's coach and head of selectors, however, had not lost sight of what Durham's ugly duckling might one day become. Full recognition had perhaps been put on ice, but Fletcher and Graveney did not want Harmison to feel abandoned.

"I think Harmy benefits from my close connections with Durham," says Graveney. "I was able to relay messages either directly or through the medical staff. During the period when he was overlooked for others he was either injured or coming back from injury. There were serious doubts about his ability to bowl. His injuries were definitely related to the number of overs he had bowled. As selectors you have to ask yourself: 'Can he get through a five-day game?' It was as simple a question as that. The number of wickets he had taken was irrelevant. You could disregard county cricket. His ability was obvious.

"All we were looking for from him was a sustained period of being injury free, so that you could put your hand on your heart and tell him: 'If you get through this, you're back in the frame.' It's pointless considering people, particularly at the start of their careers, who are concerned about being injured or aren't in the best possible form. It was just a question of picking that right time.

"I would speak to Geoff quite a lot. You get feedback. He would have been desperate to convince the medical staff that he was ready to play when he probably wasn't, only to get injured again. It was a frustrating period for him."

Cook says it was a credit to the England management "that they kept dangling the carrot". At the end of 2001, the carrot would be a place in England's first intake for their National Academy.

The Academy, to be based at Loughborough, was modelled on its Australian equivalent, an institution with a proven record of identifying and fast-tracking players of the calibre of Warne, McGrath and Ricky Ponting into Test cricket. The England selectors, who had set themselves the audacious target of producing the world's best side by 2007, made sure of giving the venture every chance of success by recruiting former Australia wicket-keeper Rod Marsh as the Academy's first head. Marsh, who had once famously referred to English bowlers as "pie throwers", had carried out the same role with extraordinary success in his home country.

Marsh's intended aim was not to transform every one of his charges into Test players but rather to give them all that chance, while unearthing a handful of players who would enjoy long-term careers at the top level. His no-nonsense, keen-eyed approach, not dissimilar to that of his fellow countryman Boon, would suit Harmison perfectly.

The squad, with players aged from 19 to 24, assembled at Sandhurst's Royal Military Academy for a demanding week of character- and team-building sessions. The squad then flew out to Adelaide, where they would stay at the Australian

Academy's facilities for a 16-week stint interrupted only by a Christmas break.

Abrahams, who had first come across Harmison before his ill-fated 1996-7 tour of Pakistan, was now one of Marsh's coaching assistants. "He had matured quite a lot as a person. He was married, and he had his first daughter as well," he recalls. Harmison, at 22, now also believed that he belonged in such company. Several other squad members he counted as friends. Flintoff was on the flight to Australia. Glamorgan's Simon Jones and fellow fast bowler Tudor were also in the squad, as were Key, Ian Bell and Andrew Strauss.

Harmison, however, still had much to learn about his chosen career.

"One thing we do at the Academy is to address the cricketing side, what it means to be a professional and Test cricketer, and how to deal with the media," Abrahams says. "I hope he thinks that his experience on the Academy did help him in that respect. We do presentation skills. We do standing up and talking to people. He'll admit his first effort was abysmal.

"You have to talk for a minute on your favourite subject and Harmy got the giggles. He looked at Flintoff and he sat down after 15 seconds. But by the end he was talking about anything."

The Academy also addressed nutrition, but a commitment to a correct diet was not Harmison's strong point either. His friends from Ashington remember him eating constantly, forever fuelling up on his favourite burgers, pies and junk food.

Harmison made an immediate impression on his coaches, however, with his work ethic. His natural attributes were well known but his appetite for hard work – when he saw the point of what he was being asked to do, or found it fun – had not been fully appreciated. Harmison had good lungs, good wheels and plenty of heart. The stay at Sandhurst included army-style 10-mile hikes with heavy backpacks, while in Adelaide there would be tough swimming, gym and even boxing sessions. Several of the squad were physically sick during the workouts. Anybody moaning at the early morning starts and the less than luxurious accommodation would have got short shrift, but Harmison was not among them.

"He would bowl and bowl for you, whatever the conditions, and he was happy doing that. There was a lot more about him. He was learning quickly and taking things on board. He didn't shout his mouth off like one or two players, but he does think about his game and what is required," recalls Abrahams. "The ones that you look for in our job are the ones that have the potential and that special ability to succeed at the highest level. There are loads of good players but which one will be successful coping with the pressure of playing, say, at the WACA? And which one can affect games for England? Flintoff was already like that when I saw him in the Lancashire Under-14s. He was awesome. And Harmy was similar. He had that raw pace which was frightening.

"He was an easy lad to like as well, and it was easy to want to help him. He wasn't arrogant, and he still isn't. He has a special talent, but he doesn't take advantage of it. He will do things for you, too, which people perhaps don't recognise. He's the one who talks to me when I go up to Durham; he's the one who drags me in for lunch."

Considering the travails of the previous two seasons, the Australia trip was an unexpected triumph for Harmison. The Academy played eleven games in all, mostly against state second teams, winning eight and losing two. The most high-profile game was against Australia's Commonwealth Bank-sponsored Cricket Academy. The Australians were younger than their English counterparts, but the match still carried symbolic importance for Marsh and his players. They won by an innings. Strauss, Key and Bell all made centuries, while Harmison was the most successful bowler with seven wickets.

His performances on the second leg of the tour – he began with eight wickets at the Melbourne Cricket Club (MCG) against a Victoria Second XI in early January – were all the more remarkable considering that he had been on the brink of backing out of the return trip after Christmas.

His wife Hayley had joined him in Australia in December. After that, along with the rest of the squad, they flew back to Britain for a Christmas break But when the time came to return to Australia, Harmison did not want to go. As he had done with England A, his bags packed and his blazer on, he backed out at the last minute. It was as if he could not physically walk out of the door.

His friends, having said their goodbyes the day before, were surprised to find him still at home. He phoned the England management to try to explain. However, they were already well aware of Harmison's background and history.

He was allowed to take stock for a couple more days after the rest of the party set off before Abrahams went to collect him. Perhaps, in retrospect, that time was as important as any period in his career. Harmison had a fundamental decision to take and he took it. When Abrahams arrived "he was all packed and ready. Neither of us ever mentioned or talked about not going. We got in the car and drove to the airport at Newcastle and flew down to London. There was absolutely no problem at all and we left for Australia."

Marsh later showed a sensitive appreciation of his young bowler when deciding that Harmison, having spearheaded the attack in every game without a break since the squad returned to Australia, would not be needed for the last few matches. Marsh would later give him rave reviews, along with Key, Bell and Jones. As fate would have it, Harmison injured himself in his last game in any case. Bowling against South Australia's Second XI, he freakishly caught his thumb in his pocket while bowling and partially dislocated his shoulder, sidelining him for several months.

CHAPTER SIX

HOMESICKNESS

Homesickness is not exactly a new phenomenon. It was first identified as a condition in the 17th century. Wars and power struggles were a regular feature in the Europe of the time. Switzerland tried to avoid conflict through defensive treaties with more powerful neighbours while exporting its fighters, famed for their loyalty and courage, across the continent, often to the highest bidder.

Battle-hardened as they were, however, the stress of a Swiss mercenary's life sometimes translated itself into a chronic, even debilitating, longing for home. A Swiss physician, Johannes Hofer, was the first to diagnose what he called "nostalgia" or "nostalgic disease" (derived from the Greek 'nostos', meaning to return home or to one's native land, and 'algia', meaning pain, suffering or grief). His dissertation was to introduce the word 'homesickness' into European languages. The German term 'heimweh' translates literally as 'home-woe'. Writings of the period suggested that the elite of Swiss fighters, armed with pikes and razor-sharp halbards and a terrifying prospect in their burnished helmets and breastplates, could occasionally be moved to depression or desertion at the sound of yodelling or the clanging of cowbells. Attempts were even made to ban Alpine songs anywhere near the mercenaries' encampments.

Hofer blamed animal spirits in the inner parts of the brain for causing "frequent contemplations of the Fatherland".

Other studies suggested that the descent from high to low altitude might be disorientating the Swiss. Some of their troops were restrained in high towers or strapped into swivelling chairs in an attempt to counter the change of air pressure. Bloodletting became a favourite cure.

Later research into 'The Swiss Disease' was to argue that its causes might be as much cultural as physiological, with peoples from remote, self-reliant communities and clans more liable to suffer. The kilted fighting men from the Scottish Highlands, renowned for their savage ferocity on the battlefield, were also reputed to be vulnerable in quieter, more contemplative moments.

The world's military have continued to struggle with the issue ever since. It was discussed during the Napoleonic wars and the American Civil War in the 19th century, when it was considered a mild form of insanity. Today, regular mail from home is regarded as an essential support for troop morale and ranked almost as highly as fresh supplies of ammunition and food. The United States army tries to recreate familiar reminders of home town life in its military camps abroad.

Prominent figures in civilian life also appear to have been sufferers. The 19th century author Emily Bronte, regarded as a fierce and independent character within her own environment, was transformed into a far less confident individual whenever she ventured far from her beloved Yorkshire moors. She left her home town of Haworth on only a handful of occasions during her life, each time more reluctantly than before. Most of her biographers conclude that she suffered from an acute form of homesickness.

In more modern times, homesickness appears to have become less worthy of popular debate. It is commonly associated with the young and with growing up. Boarding school pupils and students are supposed to be the only valid victims and even they are encouraged to grow up and avoid wallowing in self-pity.

Universities take a more broad-minded view, offering counselling services to students. Research shows that between 50 and 70 per cent of them, leaving home for the first time, suffer some form of homesickness. The huge majority quickly conquer the problem but a few never cope and fail to complete their first terms. Some experts suggest that homesickness can even be more difficult to cope with than the finality of bereavement, since there is always the possibility of retreat, with families never more than a phone call or a train ride away.

Psychologists today tend to avoid the term homesickness. It does not appear as an entry in one of their bibles, the *Diagnostic and Statistical Manual of the American Psychiatric Association.* Extreme cases are more often linked to other anxiety conditions, such as agoraphobia, which is not merely, as commonly believed, a fear of open spaces. "Literally, the word means fear of the market place, so it can be fear of crowds," says Professor Roger Baker, consultant clinical psychologist with the Dorset Healthcare NHS Trust and the author of *Understanding Panic Attacks and Overcoming Fear.* "It can also be a fear of being in situations where the sufferer does not feel safe, provoking an urge to escape to a secure place which, in most cases, translates as home." Charles Darwin was a sufferer of some such phobia, preferring to stay home for much of his later life rather than risk panic attacks in social situations.

Other people, says Baker, can experience "separation anxiety", where the fear is of being away from a person rather than home. All such sufferers, he says, "are normal people with normal lives. They're not impaired, they just have these pockets of phobias".

Harmison was barely 18, the age of many first-year students, when he left home for Pakistan. His close-knit background must have meant an immense cultural shock, his sense of isolation heightened by his lack of immediate friends within the England Under-19 squad. An attack of homesickness would have been natural enough. As Abrahams points out, other squad members would have struggled as well, as they do on most tours. Some sort of counselling might have helped, if anybody had been brave enough to admit needing it. But men, according to psychologists, sometimes find it difficult to do so in case they are perceived as weak.

"I don't know what the psychology of it was, but even before he was married he did have a problem being away from home, there's no doubt about it," says Geoff Cook. "He felt it on the county circuit and when he was off travelling with the England A team or the England Under-19s. They were genuine problems."

Early on, the English press must have been bemused by the idea of a homesick fast bowler. There were the inevitable jokes. Durham and England were desperately in need of a bowler with Harmison's obvious ability and the last thing they needed was a sheep masquerading in wolf's clothing.

Fast bowlers are often caricatured as fearless, broad-shouldered and maniacally aggressive, armed with the one intent of inflicting physical and psychological damage on their foes. There is nothing on the cricket field more elemental and enthralling than a primitive, full-blooded confrontation between fast bowler and batsman.

One particular clash, between South African Allan Donald and England opening batsman Michael Atherton, has gone down in sporting folklore. The sense of danger was almost palpable at Trent Bridge, that July day in 1998. Atherton, indeed, seemed to be fighting for his very survival, not just his wicket, as Donald's howitzers rained down on him. The glaring Donald, convinced that Atherton should have been given out caught behind at a key moment, responded with such venomous fury that it is tempting to think he might almost have left himself open to criminal charges had he managed to injure his opponent.

The bowler thus plays the role of bull, repeatedly charging his quarry, while the batsman, the matador, attempts to avoid mortal injury.

As a young man, Harmison failed to fit the caricature in most respects. However competitive and determined he was to succeed on the inside, outwardly he looked more choir boy than brawler. He was quiet. True, he could aim a cricket ball at someone's head at more than 90mph and was, indeed, more than willing to do so, but he rarely followed up with the traditional glower or Anglo-Saxon obscenity. Even today some opponents, perhaps fooled by his lack of overt menace, have questioned his mental toughness.

By and large, Harmison received a supportive press in his early years but there were reservations tucked away between the lines. Shortly after Harmison had made his debut in 2002 and headed off for Australia, for instance, one tabloid announced that he had "come clean" over his homesickness – come clean, as in an admission of some crime. It added, tongue firmly in cheek, that while on tour Harmison had "promised he would not be distracted by pining for Northumberland, Newcastle United and nappy-changing". Until he proved his worth, Harmison would always be wide open to such ribbing.

He is not the first modern player to miss the attractions of home and he will doubtless not be the last. International sportsmen and women, in effect, seek fame and fortune on foreign fields just as any mercenary might have done more than 300 years ago. Away for long periods, they are naturally vulnerable to feelings of isolation. In today's fast-moving, cosmopolitan world, though, there is little sympathy for –

and perhaps little understanding of – such frailties. Sports stars are perceived by many fans as well paid and cosseted, leading much-envied lives. They are to be worshipped or vilified, but certainly not pitied.

Even world champions are vulnerable. Steve Waugh was one of cricket's toughest, most successful and most single-minded of practitioners. Leading Australia to the West Indies immediately after the team's 2003 World Cup triumph, though, he said the "homesickness factor" posed more of a worry for the squad than physical fatigue. "That's the toughest thing to overcome... when you've got down time you tend to think about things more often and that will be the biggest hurdle for the side to get over. They are basically going to be overseas for four months straight. It's been very continuous and a lot of the guys in the side now have their own families, so the dynamics of the team have changed."

Golfers, like cricketers, spend ever longer periods on the road living out of suitcases, their season, too, now extending throughout the year. Miguel Angel Jimenez decided that if he could not spend as much time as he liked in his home country, then he would at least take as much of Spain with him as he could on his travels. At the 2003 Ryder Cup, he had some special requests for the European team room at Oakland Hills – an espresso machine, plentiful supplies of the finest Rioja, and Cuban cigars. "I always like to feel at home and I miss Spain," he said. "These are the things that make you happy."

Australian hammer thrower Bronwyn Eagles used similar tactics when she went to the Athens Olympics in 2004. She plastered her room with photographs of her parents and seven siblings in an effort to cope. The imposing Eagles, who won a 2001 World Championships bronze medal and a 2002 Commonwealth silver, is not the sort of woman who could be called weak. But she clearly suffered during her training camps and in the Games themselves. "I am so family orientated that being away from them really does hurt me," she said.

Lance Armstrong is another competitor few would characterise as lacking moral fibre. A cycling legend, the five-times winner of the Tour de France has shown himself capable of enduring, and indeed repeatedly conquering, one of the toughest physical challenges that sport can offer. Take him away from his children, however – as happens every year when he gears up for the Tour – and he suffers. "In three months, they change so much," he says of his youngsters. "I become desperate, they are so far away."

Cricketers have it worse than most, and must have had it worst of all in the days when full-scale tours lasted for months. These days trips are much shorter, but there are more of them and, even when playing at home, players can spend long periods away from their families. Before setting out for the 2002-3 Ashes tour, Harmison's England colleague, Matthew Hoggard, worked out that he had owned a house for two-and-a-half years and lived in it for a total of two months.

Such demands can put a huge strain on family life and relationships. For anyone prone to homesickness, it is harder still. Even before he was married and became a father, Harmison used to struggle spending time on the road. Former England team mate Alec Stewart is supportive, but is tempted to see it as a significant condition. "His life centres around his village and the working men's club, and he comes from a very close-knit family. That is all he has known, so you can understand why he finds it difficult to go to a foreign area," he says. "People knock him, but I call it an illness.

"Now he's married with two children and he misses them, as we all do with our families, but he's largely overcome it. It's still a big thing for him to say goodbye for months at a time."

The strength of Harmison's homesickness – he says he often rings home up to half-a-dozen times a day – may seem as extraordinary as it is unusual, but there is no denying his determination to defy it. His inability as a young man to pull away from his deep Ashington roots was clearly a significant threat to his cricket career. Indeed, it almost killed off the Harmison story before it had really begun.

Ultimately, however, Harmison must have known by 2002 that he would have to prove two things if he were to dismiss the issue. He would have to make sure he boarded every England flight on time in the future, and he would have to be as successful a bowler abroad as he was at home. Only then would he be able to demonstrate that he had found a way of leaving his homesickness beyond the boundary rope while performing with distinction within it. Only then would he be able to silence those who suggested he was mentally suspect.

CHAPTER SEVEN

INDIAN SUMMER, AUSTRALIAN WINTER

Steve Harmison the bowler had always come with a large-scale caveat attached, ever since he burst on to the scene as an elongated juvenile. A young man now, he still appeared to inspire excitement and mistrust in equal measure. His critics eyed him as warily as a box of explosives hissing in the midday sun, while his champions saw in him that vital piece of heavy artillery missing from England's battle lines for almost two decades. Increasingly, however, the people that mattered thought the time was coming to test him.

Youth, indeed, was about to come back into vogue in 2002, partly out of necessity. Gough, England's talisman, did not yet know it but he was on his last legs – or, in his case, knees. Having declined to tour India and been left out of the Test squad for New Zealand, his hopes of quickly re-establishing himself were dashed by a series of operations that would keep him out for most of the year and also wreck his prospects of another Ashes tour. Indeed, he had only two more Tests in him.

Caddick remained, but he was 33. Other senior England players, too, were showing signs of metal fatigue. "Dad's Army", as the team was dubbed at the start of their home season, was ready for a changing of the guard.

Harmison, fresh from his successful stint at the Academy, had come close to selection for the winter visit to New Zealand before losing out to Ormond. Now he headed the queue of heirs apparent, but injuries intervened. His shoulder dislocation had disrupted his preparations for the season and he made a lethargic start. Against Middlesex in April he took three wickets in the first innings, including that of future England batsman Strauss – a scalp that would become ever more prized in the seasons to follow – but that was about as good as it got. Soon, with a wretched piece of timing, he was sidelined by a side injury, and missed much of May and June.

By then England were well into their summer campaign, having seen off Sri Lanka 2-0 over three Tests. That success seemed to owe as much to the touring side's failure to acclimatise as to England's strengths. The home attack for the first Test at Lord's, indeed, had been more squeaking Chihuahua than slavering Rottweiler.

Caddick found himself backed up by Hoggard, a dependable fast-medium seamer of growing reputation, but with only eight Tests to his name, and two all-rounders in Dominic Cork, who at 30 would not play for England beyond that summer, and Flintoff, a player only just beginning to fulfil his promise.

It did not look like the sort of attack to blast out the Sri Lankans after their remarkable run of nine Test victories in a row and so it proved. The visitors hammered 555 for eight declared in their first innings and England, forced to follow on, were only saved by second-innings centuries from Vaughan and Butcher.

Hussain had been as disappointed with his firepower as most England supporters. Having turned the team around since the dark days of 1999, he now hankered after something special. Reviewing the Lord's match, he said: "There is a case for picking a left-arm seamer or a mystery spinner – and someone with raw pace would be nice. If pitches are going to be this flat, we need to work out how we can take 20 wickets. People have got to hold up their hands."

Tudor, offering more pace and fewer histrionics, replaced Cork for the final two Tests while Giles' left-arm spin was also re-introduced to the mix. England, better balanced, won the next two matches comprehensively. Hoggard struck a blow for the new generation with a match-winning performance in Birmingham, and Tudor did the same in the Third Test at Old Trafford.

There was another spate of injuries, however, and this time they played into Harmison's hands. By the time India arrived for the First Test in late July, Caddick and Tudor were on the physiotherapist's couch and the attack was being remodelled again. Simon Jones, who had been at the Academy in Adelaide with Harmison, had jumped past him to the front of the queue and made his debut at Lord's. He made a big impression with a spirited display as the home side won by 170 runs. Bowling with refreshing vim, he took two wickets in each innings – accounting for Virender Sehwag and VVS Laxman in the second – and hit 44 fearless runs in his one innings. It was a near-perfect start, marred only by a side strain which ruled him out of the next match... and thus the door finally opened wide for the 23-year-old Harmison at Trent Bridge. England coach Fletcher had long been a committed fan but, by nature conservative, he had wanted to cherry-pick the occasion. Now there was little choice. Had he played in 2000, the Durham bowler would have been faced by the likes of the Flower brothers, Murray Goodwin and Alastair Campbell. Instead, he would line up against the altogether more formidable Rahul Dravid, Sachin Tendulkar and Sourav Ganguly.

Right-handed batsman Robert Key, another Academy man and one of Harmison's best friends on the cricket circuit, was also selected for his debut. Thorpe, the cornerstone of the England top order, had made himself unavailable as he struggled with a disintegrating marriage. Thus Key and

Harmison became the Trent Bridge story for the English media. Jones, at Lord's, had arrived with a pre-prepared script, since his father Jeff had played for England. Harmison's stop-start career offered less obvious colour for the newspaper writers, but there was enough to work with.

The Times's Richard Hobson noted the apparent differences in temperament between Harmison and Key, suggesting self-belief would be an issue for the Durham bowler. "Harmison is far less worldly-wise," Hobson wrote. "Where Key seemed relaxed in the company of the Fourth Estate two days ago, Harmison could not hide his nerves. He twitched, scratched, and stroked his cheeks and chin while his feet beat a light tattoo against the floor. Perhaps he simply feels edgier talking to a dozen journalists than playing in front of a 15,000 crowd. At least he sounded convincing when he said he has the self-belief to bowl at Tendulkar." As for his homesickness, it said: "He has tackled the problem bravely, with the help of a psychologist, and for that alone deserves encouragement rather than mockery as he now tries to take his career forward. One of his biggest challenges will be to overcome attempts by the opposition to break his confidence."

The preview concluded with real foresight: "With England desperate for pace he is certainly worth a try. There is something of the Devon Malcolm about his style. Harmison, too, might go on to enjoy days of blinding glory, when speed and accuracy conflate... But England will need the right support bowling for the more frequent occasions when things do not click so readily."

Harmison said in interviews before the match that his homesickness was a thing of the past. Perhaps he believed it, or perhaps he had been advised to avoid the subject as best he could when addressing the media. That did not stop a report in the *Birmingham Post* referring to it. "The joke on the circuit is that he gets homesick when he walks down the road in Ashington (Jack and Bobby Charlton country) to fetch his morning newspaper," it said. "Such a natural introvert could well sink without trace in the cauldron of international cricket."

The *Daily Telegraph's* Derek Pringle also highlighted what it saw as physical and mental fragility. "Since his county debut in 1996, he has been laid low by back injury, shin splints, a dislocated shoulder and an inter-costal problem which has only just cleared up," it remarked. "He also suffers from homesickness, not an ideal malady for a professional cricketer to have, especially one expecting his second child." The *Daily Express* homed in on his dubious control of line and length. "Harmison has more varieties than Mr Heinz," Colin Bateman wrote.

Despite the levity of tone, there was real substance to all those concerns and they would have been shared in part by Fletcher and Hussain. Harmison was an exciting selection who, at his best, looked well suited to exploiting the Indian batsmen's weakness against fast, rib-cage deliveries. But it was also an audacious one or, as *The Guardian* put it: "Should Harmison play, it would represent the biggest gamble England have taken in years." His record suggested that he had "as much chance of lasting the course as Dennis Wise has of getting a Nobel peace prize. There are members at Durham who profess that they were unaware he was on the staff, so infrequently has he appeared because of injury. He is said to get homesick if he crosses the border into Yorkshire. His bowling radar makes Devon Malcolm seem pinpoint." But, it also said, he was 6ft 4ins tall, extracted bounce and had pace, adding: "He might have his work cut out but Hussain is adept at squeezing the best out of his players."

Hussain and Fletcher opted for a five-man seam attack, though even that battery would be found wanting. India opted to bat first on a true strip but with the overhead conditions favouring seam bowling. The home attack failed to capitalise. Hoggard, swinging his way to four wickets, got Wasim Jaffer for a duck but his opening partner, Virender Sehwag, made a century. Dominic Cork and Craig White were disappointingly ineffectual, while Flintoff bowled too short and with too much width.

So did Harmison. He had to wait his turn as Hussain opened with Hoggard and Cork before coming on after nine overs. Statistically, his opening spell in Test cricket was impressive – four overs, four maidens. In truth, though, he struggled to retain any control over his nerves or the ball as he sent down a high-speed concoction of bouncers and wide deliveries both sides of the wicket. As he would concede later, he only bowled maidens because the batsmen could not reach the ball. After 24 deliveries, with the batsmen barely forced to play two balls in a row, Hussain took pity and sent him back to fine leg.

He had two more spells on a rain-curtailed first day without taking a wicket. The second day was even shorter as the bad weather persisted, with only 25 overs possible. Harmison, however, finally struck after the top order had been dismissed. All-rounder Ajit Agarkar had made 34 when he cut at a short delivery and top-edged to third man where Mark Butcher dashed in and took a sprawling catch. Moments later the diminutive Parthiv Patel, who at 17 became the youngest wicket-keeper to play Test cricket, snicked a catch to Flintoff in the slips without scoring. Harmison had taken two wickets for one run in eight balls. When he also removed a slogging Harbhajan Singh on the third morning, it was three for 13 off 13, wicket to wicket, and three for 57 overall.

Harbhajan's demise produced another esoteric statistic which only the most avid of Durham supporters would have noticed. That wicket made Harmison Durham's most successful Test bowler, surpassing Simon Brown's two wickets taken in his single Test against Pakistan in 1996. Botham was the only other Durham player to have played Tests for England but had failed to take a wicket in his last two games.

India were bowled out for 357 but, considering the conditions, were probably satisfied. Vaughan led England's reply with a majestic 197 out of a total of 617 all out but the batting conditions had eased. India, facing a deficit of 260, duly batted through the fourth evening and the final day without ever looking as if they would lose, Dravid making 115, Tendulkar 92 and Ganguly 99. By the time the India captain played on to Harmison the game was already as good as dead. Harmison picked up Harbhajan again to end with five wickets for the match as the contest fizzled out.

Harmison had hardly disgraced himself – indeed Fletcher saw much to admire and suggested that Harmison and Jones, one offering bounce to the other's skid, could perhaps one day emulate the Caddick-Gough alliance. But, with Caddick and Tudor fit again, Harmison was dropped for the next match at Headingley, which England lost, and did not appear in the starting line-up again as the four-match series was drawn 1-1.

Botham criticised the decision not to give Harmison a longer run, but in truth he had not done quite enough to convince. England wicket-keeper Alec Stewart remembers Harmison's debut as a mixed performance. "When he got it right, he was a real handful, and when he didn't, it could go anywhere," he said.

In any case, it turned out to be a series for the batsmen. Vaughan amassed 615 runs at an average of 102.5, adding another 195 at The Oval. Dravid slipstreamed him with 602 runs, the highest by any Indian against England. He averaged 100.33. Both players passed 1,000 Test runs in 2002 during the Fourth Test.

Dravid says that the Indians had been impressed with Harmison. "He definitely made a good impression on the team. I remember we had a chat in the dressing room since he was a new bowler to us. Sourav had faced him for Lancashire and warned us that he was quick. The general consensus was that he was potentially a very good bowler. He had pace and could hurry you, and then there was the bounce. We all thought once he got his act together and bowled in the right areas he was going to be a handful. He probably bowled two lengths at that stage, too short and then too full to compensate.

"But I have played him since, in the one-dayers, and he has really come on. What he has done is brilliant. There is no doubt he is now one of the premier bowlers in world cricket. I haven't played him enough in Tests to make a full assessment, but I think the main problem would be getting forward to him. When the ball comes from that height it's not easy to drive. You tend to hang back a lot. And when it's doing a bit, it's a problem.

"I played a bit against Ambrose early in my career and they are similar in a lot of ways, particularly the bounce. But Harmison is quicker."

Dravid would meet Harmison at close quarters around two years later, at the 2004 ICC awards, when the Indian was named Player of the Year and the Englishman came third in the poll. "To have such an impact in such a short period of time obviously tells you that when he gets it right he is going to have a huge amount of success," adds Dravid. "I remember watching him struggle in Australia on television in 2002-3. If somebody had told me that, in 15 months, he would become as successful as he has been, I probably wouldn't have believed it. I guess he wouldn't have believed it either. He's a nice bloke too, a very nice chap – quiet and friendly."

Shortly after Trent Bridge, Harmison went off to watch Newcastle United play at St James' Park. While he was at the match, his car was broken into. Perhaps the thief had been less impressed than Fletcher and thought that the Durham bowler might end up being a one-Test wonder, for he stole his bat and his cricket whites, but his England cap was left behind on the seat.

Returning to Durham, Harmison wound up with 26 County Championship wickets at 32.15 and just one five-wicket haul. But the highlight of the year was yet to come. Within a month of his first Test, and with India having left England, attention was already turning to the Ashes.

No England player who went on the 2002-3 tour to Australia is ever likely to forget it. It must rank among the most ill-starred cricket trips ever undertaken. It began badly, then got progressively worse. England, hauled up the Test rankings by Hussain and Fletcher, set out in hope but had been reduced to a chaotic shambles within a few weeks. If Harmison had been hoping for a quiet induction, he could not have chosen a worse tour. If he lacked the resolve and maturity to make it as a top-class cricketer, those Australians would surely find him out.

The player himself was confident that he could now cope with being away from Ashington. In an interview with Mike Dickinson of the *Daily Mail*, he said: "I'm not going to pretend that it is something I am over or probably ever will be, but it would not stop me going away with England. It is my dream to play Test cricket. Everyone has strengths and weaknesses and maybe that is one of my weaknesses, but I would be surprised if half the England team don't suffer from it at some time. It is fine when you are playing, but it affects you more on rest days. I did 13 and a half weeks last winter, so that shows I can cope with it."

Hussain remembers his first meeting with Harmison,

several years before. "There were rumours about him not liking touring and being homesick. We had a training camp up in Manchester, for the England squad and anyone on the periphery. I was expecting to see this weird, shy, introvert and instead I saw big Harmy come along. He was just a very nice lad. I took to him immediately. He was very down to earth. He kept himself to himself but whenever anyone got on the subject of football he would come into his own. He and Alec (Stewart) were always talking about Newcastle and Chelsea.

"And I thought: 'This lad isn't that bad, he seems a very balanced young man.' And he was certainly more balanced than some of the guys we had around the England team at that stage, the Caddicks and Tufnells and the like! When I became captain he was someone I immediately wanted to look at, and when Duncan came on board he said the same."

Harmison and Jones would be selected for Australia ahead of the more experienced Tudor. England's first-choice attack, most commentators agreed, would consist of Gough, Caddick, Hoggard and Flintoff but the two young quicks, with one Test apiece, were promising wild cards well suited to Australian conditions. Ian Botham had no doubts.

"Botham was a big fan of his. He was on at me all of the time, saying: 'Get Harmy in the side,'" says Hussain. "But I knew what mattered was the way we handled Harmy. He needed handling with care. It's about man management with Steve.

"He was so raw. We knew there was a lot of work to do – it wasn't going to happen in three weeks. But it wasn't a gamble. We needed him and we needed Jones because medium pace will only get you so far. You need mystery spin, metronomic accuracy like McGrath or Pollock, and you need pace."

To have any chance of avoiding an eighth successive Ashes series defeat, Hussain had said before departure, his men would need luck off the pitch as well as on it. "If we can get the bowlers fit," he said, "I think we've got a really good chance, the best chance against them for a long time."

England had begun to earn a reputation as a side who made up for lack of star quality with a cussed refusal to give way. Australia, though, fresh from crushing nearest rivals South Africa 5-1 and routing Pakistan, were widely regarded as the best side ever to have played the game. Man for man, it was a mismatch. Good fortune would be required, and in good measure.

Instead, things took a dive even before English bags had been packed. Thorpe, a close Hussain ally who had been riding shotgun for the top-order batsmen for years, withdrew at the last moment after months of personal turmoil. Thorpe's on-going concerns over his children, following his marriage break-up, would not have been lost on Harmison. His wife Hayley was expecting their second child in December, by which time Harmison would be on the other side of the world.

The England captain – who would also become a father for the second time during the trip but whose wife flew out to Australia with him for the birth – must also have been prone to a few doubts as the tour began. Several of his senior players had been selected despite recent injuries. Gough had not played for 14 months and had undergone three knee operations, but was regarded as too influential to leave behind. Flintoff had not played for two months after a double hernia operation. He could not even run when he boarded the plane at Heathrow. Vaughan was just back from knee surgery.

The tour curtain-raiser at Lilac Hill was little more than a one-day knock-about but Hussain wanted an early statement of intent. Instead, among the gum trees along the banks of the river Swan outside Perth, England crashed to a 58-run defeat against an Australian Cricket Board (ACB) squad including the venerable David Hookes. Fringe Western Australia all-rounder Kade Harvey blitzed 114 off 88 balls. Harmison, meanwhile, unaccustomed to the white ball, his head ringing after that early fall while fielding and his wrist-position awry, sent down those infamous seven leg-side wides in a row.

"I remember taking him off after that over and keeping him away from the boundary where there was lots of abuse, with people shouting: 'Wide, wide!' at him," says Hussain.

According to David Graveney, in those days Harmison trusted the white ball as much as he trusted a hand grenade.

The Australian press, keen to magnify every sign of weakness, delighted over the early gift. Malcolm Conn of *The Australian* already had doubts about Harmison. "I had interviewed both him and Jones before the game. Speaking to them and watching them operate, you just got the feeling that Harmison was a big lost puppy. He had a bit of a reputation for being a bit soft and homesick. He struck me as one of those blokes who would have been happier leaning against the bar talking about Newcastle United. He didn't seem to have a feel for touring the world and playing the game.

"Jones had the pedigree of his father playing at international level. He spoke with real intensity and passion about the game and his hero, Allan Donald. Harmison had no cricketers as heroes. His heroes were soccer players. He had very little cricket background or history, and he seemed to have very little enthusiasm for the game. It was almost as if he had been brought along by default.

"During the match, we were laughing in the press box and so were the crowd. It wasn't nasty humour, it was just good-natured, belly-aching laughter. Everyone was feeling fairly relaxed. It just reinforced that the Poms would be hopeless again.

"Among the English journos, some were saying 'This kid's got a bit' and others were going: 'Oh no, here we go again.' For us, it was just another day and another reason for writing off the Poms. That kid Harvey, who smashed them all over the place, was a serviceable one-day all-rounder who played a bit of four-day cricket. But if you walked down the street, nine out of 10 people would never have heard of him."

At least England avoided defeat in a two-day warm-up match against Western Australia, although they were given another fright when reduced to 126 for eight, "former Perth window cleaner" Callum Thorp taking four for 58. The dismissive tone of the press coverage was already set. When Craig White was called up from playing grade cricket in Adelaide as injury cover for Flintoff shortly before the First Test, one report began: "Clear the hospital beds in Brisbane – the England cricket team is arriving next week."

Harmison's difficulties were noted again. Dropping short, he went for 89 off 19 overs for a single wicket. His chances of an early Test berth had already gone. "He's struggled, he would be the first to say that," Hussain said. "But look, he's a young lad, he's very raw, and no one has said Steve Harmison is the answer to all our problems."

The bowler himself conceded that he was hurting. "If you had asked me at the end of October, I would quite happily have come home early," he said later.

Alec Stewart, whose wife originates from a Durham pit village, says there were times when Harmison appeared to be struggling mentally but he seemed to cope.

"He was down, inwardly. Outwardly, he's quiet anyway and that's quite a good asset to have. If Darren Gough, who's noisy as anything, had gone quiet, you would have known. But Harmy would just sit quietly with Flintoff and Key. Those guys had a big influence on that tour. There wasn't outwardly a huge difference in him. He just gets on with it.

He's the same when he gets five-for. I think it is fantastic to have a nice level way about yourself, whether you succeed or fail."

And despite his early problems, according to Stewart, Harmison remained a fearsome, if inconsistent, prospect. "I pay him this compliment," he says. "When we had nets, Duncan would put down the name of the batters and bowlers in each. Everyone wanted to see if they had copped Harmy in their net. The nets are quite claustrophobic and then you've got this great big bloke, who may just be bowling off 21 yards anyway... Normally you come out of a net feeling great, having middled a few. When you are netting against him, it's just a case of coming out and feeling you've survived."

A second warm-up against a stronger Western Australia side went better, Hussain leading from the front with a century. Harmison began finding some form but it was Jones who caught the eye, taking five for 78 in the second innings. Set 135 to win off 20 overs, England fell one shot short with five wickets left.

Vaughan, rated at 75 per cent fit after his knee rehabilitation, was selected for the final warm-up game against Queensland, but the touring team failed to fire again. Jones was preferred to Harmison while Flintoff was introduced to the fray. If Harmison had any advice on how to bowl at his Durham colleague Martin Love, it did not work. Dropped four times, Love scored 250 out of a total of 582. To rub it in, one Queensland batsman was caught on the eastern bank of Allan Border Field off a six, the spectator finding time to put down a meat pie before completing the catch. Vaughan provided some cheer with a century but Flintoff pulled up stiff. Tudor, in Australia with the Academy, joined the squad with less than 72 hours before the start of the series.

SHOULD I STAY OR SHOULD I GO? Steve Harmison contemplating the attractions of home. It's a look his England team-mates have got to know well.

Empics

Empics

FOR THE HIGH JUMP: Ramnaresh Sarwan (above left) is hit on the helmet, and Brian Lara takes evading action, as Harmison dishes out the chin music in the NatWest series against the West Indies in 2004.

GOT HIM! Harmison celebrates the dismissal of Australia's Andrew Symonds (facing page) during the ICC Trophy semi-final at Edgbaston in 2004.

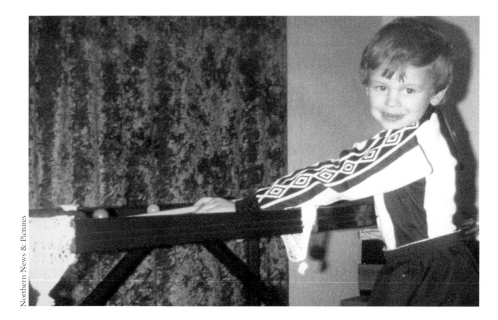

HOME GAME:
Playing pool aged 5,
wearing his beloved
Newcastle United
shirt, in the family
house in Ashington.

STREET KID:
Steve in 1984
wearing his father's
Great North Run
shirt.

MEDAL CRICKETERS: Steve (back row, far left) with the Ashington under-15s who were county champions in 1995. His brother James is on the front row, far right.

HARMY ARMY: Five of the Harmison family in the Ashington Third XI which won the Ian Appleby Cup in 1996. Steve is back row, second left, uncle Melvin fourth left and father Jim fifth left. On the front row, brother James is second left and uncle Kevin far right.

ACTION MAN: Harmison bowling for Durham against Gloucestershire in 1998 (above). The picture on the right shows the finished article, as Harmison bowls at Sarwan on the 2004 tour to the West Indies. His devastating return of 7 for 12 in Jamaica swung the series for England.

Northern News & Pictures

HOME IS THE HERO: Harmison faces a barrage of reporters as he returns to Ashington after his triumph on England's tour to the West Indies in 2004.

The picture on the right shows him holding the Npower Test series trophy, won in the West Indies.

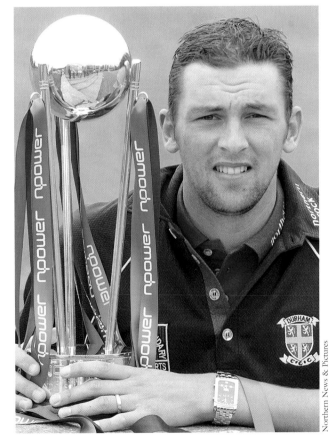

Northern News & Pictures

BIG FRIENDLY GIANTS: Harmison and his best mate in the England team, Andrew Flintoff, celebrate victory over India in the NatWest challenge in 2004.

The First Test at the Gabba would prove an unmitigated disaster. With Gough and Flintoff unavailable, Jones played. With the second session barely underway, however, the young Welshman was already heading for hospital with a ruptured anterior cruciate ligament in his right knee after an attempted sliding gather in the outfield went wrong as his studs caught in the turf. Facing re-constructive surgery, Jones would not play for England again for another 14 months.

At least he managed seven overs and a wicket during the series. Gough and Flintoff would not even get on the field. Caddick would also miss one Test and Ashley Giles missed three. Hoggard played three of the five. Those six bowlers would have hoped to offer their captain a potential total of 150 days of hard Test toil in Australia but managed less than a third of that between them. To make matters worse, the replacements fared little better. For misfortune, no one could match Chris Silverwood. Flown in to bolster the squad for the final three Tests, the Yorkshire quick stuck out his chest, promised to meet fire with fire and vowed to grasp his opportunity. He took to the field in Perth, damaged ankle ligaments after bowling eight balls, and returned home.

Hussain and Fletcher might have broken down themselves had they realised what was to come. Things were bad enough after day one of the series. Australia, put in by Hussain on a hunch that the Brisbane pitch might offer early seam movement, ended the day on 364 for two, with Ponting scoring a century and Matthew Hayden, offered three lives, pummelling the boundary boards without mercy.

England fought back and began their reply brightly but none of their batsmen were able to push on. By the fourth day they were facing defeat. To compound their misery, it was announced that Gough would fly home, ruled out of the next three months as well as the World Cup.

Australia administered the last rites quickly. Hayden added

103 to his first-innings 197 in front of his home crowd – he was batting, according to Steve Waugh, "almost as well as anyone in the history of the game" – and the touring side, set 464 to win, subsided pitifully to 79 all out in 28.2 overs.

A match against Australia A sandwiched between the first two Tests offered little respite. Harmison, Tudor and Flintoff looked an intriguing new-ball attack on paper, but Love ripped up the script with another undefeated double century. Only in Australia could a batsman score 451 runs without being dismissed against Test opponents and still be overlooked. Harmison bowled short and wide and failed to take a wicket. England were then skittled for 183 – they lasted 19 minutes less than Love had done – and followed on. It took 174 not out from Robert Key to avoid more English blushes. John Crawley, meanwhile, a batting limpet rather than linchpin, received a crack on the hip and was ruled out of the Second and Third Tests.

Hussain had to keep believing, despite his dwindling resources. At least he had no worries about throwing Harmison into the deep end.

"When I took over and Duncan came in, there was a problem with English cricket – everybody looked at what people couldn't do. They'd say Caddick was a bad tourist, Tufnell was a bad tourist, Thorpe just gets his runs – he's not interested in anyone else," says Hussain. "Everything was a negative. In the end I sat down in selection meetings and said that I was sick of hearing what people couldn't do. Steve Harmison can bowl quick, he can get bounce that no other bowler gets.

"There were no problems whatsoever with his attitude in Australia. He was the sort of person I wanted around the England dressing room – people who didn't just say: 'Botham says this, or another person says that'. I wanted people who give and take. I have always found that with

Steve. He was the kind of lad that, if you gave him something, you would get a lot back.

"Perhaps he is a bit different from most people, but the fortunate thing is that I was also a bit different. I wasn't Alec Stewart or Graham Gooch. It might look like that on the screen, but for me the cricket wasn't the be-all-and-end-all, in as much as I wasn't thinking: 'Oh good, it's October, there's a tour coming up and we've got four months away from home!' At that stage I had a young family myself. I suppose if I had been 21 and was going to the Caribbean, then I would have thought: 'Crickey, why doesn't this lad want to go away from home?' But when I took over I fully understood.

"When you are at the top level you are going to have all sorts. This is what some people like Gooch did not quite understand as captain – and he still doesn't completely – that you are going to have a complete spectrum of people.

"I found Harmy a good egg. I'd ring him up or he'd ring me up, and we would meet in the bar. I have always liked him. I like his loyalty, not just to me but to his fellow players. It is a big thing for Fletcher and it is a big thing for me."

Hussain remembers one particular incident, early in 2003 at the end of the World Cup, when Flintoff and Harmison had gone out for a drink. Flintoff had got drunk and was barred from attending a sponsor's function. "Duncan and I were trying to get the drink culture out of the team and we dragged both of them in. We dragged Harmy in before Freddie, and he would not have a bad word said about his mate. When we chatted to Freddie he was still half pissed the next morning. But Harmy kept saying Flintoff had had a couple of beers and that was it. I remember walking away and thinking: 'Good on you.'"

Harmison was to return to the headlines in the run-up to the Second Test but, as at Lilac Hill, it was for the wrong reasons. Bowling his first ball at Giles in the Adelaide nets, he broke the spinner's left wrist. Giles, England's most successful bowler in the First Test with six wickets, joined the queue at the airport check-in desk. Now the touring party would go into the second match with just one experienced bowler in Caddick.

By now bickering had begun inside the camp over injuries, with Flintoff's failure to get fit the main source of frustration. Some blamed the player, but former England captain Michael Atherton, writing in *The Sunday Telegraph,* said the medical side of the team's preparations bordered on the amateurish and argued that the all-rounder's rehabilitation had been mismanaged.

It was left to Vaughan to offer England some cheer. His 177 helped the touring side to 295 for four on the first day in Adelaide while Australia grassed six catches. England's ascendancy, though, was short-lived.

Their last six wickets were swept away for 47 runs as the world champions resumed normal service. Harmison worked manfully but without success as part of an attack comprising Caddick, Hoggard, all-rounder White and off-spinner Richard Dawson. He enjoyed little fortune. Hayden smashed his third ball to gully but was dropped. There was also an edge from Damien Martyn to Stewart's right at a comfortable height, only for the keeper to fail to lay a glove on the ball, while Waugh was put down at leg gully.

By the end of the third day England were again heading for defeat after conceding a 210-run first-innings deficit. Ponting did most of the damage with a magnificent 154. Harmison at least had the satisfaction of removing Martin for 95, ending a 242-run stand and taking his first Ashes wicket before finishing with two for 106.

The game was over in almost as ignominious circumstances as the First Test, the home side sealing victory by an innings and 51 runs with more than a day to spare. This time England managed 159 in their second knock. It had been a wretched performance on all fronts. The fact that the rain arrived next day, suggesting that England might have escaped had they survived one more hour on the fourth evening, did not lighten the squad's mood.

And still the injuries piled up. Within hours of the humiliation Caddick, suffering from back spasms, went from physio's couch to hospital for a scan. Steroid injections were prescribed and he was ruled out of the Third Test.

If the first two Tests had been one-sided, the Perth encounter promised to be bloodier still. The contrast in experience, never mind the quality, of the two bowling attacks, was almost risible. England's bowlers boasted 20 caps between them – Harmison with two, Silverwood with five (the last of which has been almost two years before), Dawson with four and Tudor with nine. Australia's frontliners, led by the incomparable Glenn McGrath and Shane Warne, boasted 255.

Silverwood, Tudor and back-up all-rounder White had not even been original tour selections. Of that attack, indeed, only Harmison continued to feature as an England bowler over the next two years.

At least he had something to look forward to this time. The Perth deck was being talked up as the fastest in Australia for two decades.

England won the toss and little else besides as they were skittled for 185 on their way to an innings-and-48-run defeat inside three days. The Ashes had been decided in less than 11 days of cricket. Silverwood's Test career ended with him limping off on the first evening, while Tudor said goodbye to England on the third day as he was stretchered off to hospital, his eyebrow sliced open after being smashed on the helmet by fast bowler Brett Lee.

The game would be almost as painful for Harmison, psychologically rather than physically. With Silverwood sidelined, Harmison bowled with hostility on the first evening, braving an Australian onslaught to remove Hayden. After a short spell on the second morning, however, the Durham bowler suddenly lost his bearings. Three times during his fifth over he lost his run-up and ran through the crease as the crowd got increasingly restless. He was taken off for more than an hour but, on his return, the problem soon returned as he bailed out of two more deliveries. Two balls after lunch and he hopped, skipped, jumped and stuttered to a stop again as he ran up to bowl.

"It was quite a traumatic time for him, he literally couldn't get his run-up in," recalls Hussain. "I went over and would be talking about anything else: 'What are we going to do for lunch, Harmy?' or: 'Don't worry Harmy, if you don't know when you are going to deliver it, Damien Martyn certainly doesn't. Just run up and let it go and don't worry about it.'" Hussain was criticised by some television commentators for over-meddling but he is dismissive of such remarks: "I had to do the man-management. It was arm-around-shoulder time."

Later, Harmison said that Hussain's help had been crucial in keeping him going. "That was the first time in my life when I have thought, 'Please don't throw me the ball, I don't want to bowl' – but his encouragement was priceless," he told Mike Walters of the *Daily Mirror*. "One or two players have criticised Nasser for nagging his bowlers too much, but his handling of the situation was brilliant.

"I was struggling, but he refused to take me off. He just said, 'Keep going, you'll get it back' and tried to take my mind off it."

Stewart, behind the stumps, likens it to the golfing "yips", adding: "I felt huge sympathy for him. I could understand him wanting the earth to swallow him up. There he was, on a big stage in front of around 20,000 people at the WACA, playing against the best side in the world. It was on television as well, so it hurt. If you've gone like that, and I've spoken to others who've had it, you can't even remember how to start your run-up. Do you set off with both feet together, the left or the right? Nothing can be worse than wondering how you are going to get to the wicket, let alone where the ball is going to go."

Somehow Harmison rediscovered his equilibrium. He finished well, with a seven-over spell, continuing to bowl at around 93mph. He hit Lee's helmet and suffered another dropped catch. The series had gone but Stewart thinks that the Durham bowler's stubborn refusal to give in, stop bowling or fake an injury and slink off the field, was a key development. "He came through it, which shows the strength of character that he has. He dealt with it and I think that set him up."

Waugh ended the Third Test celebrating a personal milestone as he equalled Allan Border's Australian record of 32 Test wins as captain – he would surpass it in a matter of days – while Hussain ended it celebrating nothing at all. Tudor's exit had been the perfect image of Hussain's team – down and flat out.

"We were embarrassingly poor... we have just been left beaten, battered and bruised by this," said Hussain. "We have been carrying a lot of injuries, but we were just not good enough."

To make it worse Waugh rubbed it in by musing on the ease of it all. Recent series wins had felt hollow, he said. "We would like to come up against a side that would really get stuck in and play tough Test match cricket and make it really tough to win."

England's quick bowlers were to do their best to satisfy Waugh's competitive instincts over the last two Tests.

Harmison's performance in Melbourne, indeed, saved his tour. One of his overs to Waugh would get far more deserved attention than that errant 14-baller at the start of the trip.

Harmison, though, went into the game after yet another own goal, forcing the team's wicket-keeper to miss the Melbourne match. "His bowling had bruised my hands horribly, especially the right one. I had had the problem for a couple of years but he certainly flared it up," says Stewart. But at least Australia had significant problems of their own this time, with Warne missing the game with a shoulder injury.

One-way traffic resumed on the first day, Hayden and Langer making centuries to take the home side to 356 for three. Langer went on to make a Test-best 250 out of a total of 551 for six, while England crumbled to 270 all out and followed on. White led the defiance with 85 not out before being ruled out of bowling for six weeks with a side muscle tear. Vaughan, however, made 145 in the second innings to at least take the game into a fifth day as Australia were set 107 to win.

Few expected much entertainment at the MCG on that final morning. England only had two fit fast bowlers left on the field. Harmison, however, suddenly found an extra yard of pace and, occasionally, an extra foot of length to inject real and totally unexpected drama into the finale. Caddick had dismissed Hayden, hooking, with the very first ball of the day, before Ponting, hitting out, gloved Harmison behind. Three balls later, Harmison also got rid of Martyn, edging behind, and Australia were 58 for three. A little more luck and England might have stolen the unlikeliest of victories.

The excitement reached a crescendo in the Durham bowler's seventh over. Caddick had cracked Langer on the helmet and Waugh had already been cut in two by a couple of seaming deliveries from Harmison in scratching four runs together when, trying to get out of the way of a lifter, he feathered a catch behind. Substitute wicket-keeper James Foster put his hands in the air but failed to appeal. The bowler and fielders looked at each other, as if not quite sure what had happened, then looked up at the giant television screen at the ground. The replay confirmed the edge, prompting a belated appeal, but by then umpire Dave Orchard had ordered play on. Next ball, Waugh drove off the back foot to Hussain, who grasped a low catch and began celebrating as the Australia captain headed for the pavilion. Waugh, though, was called back. Orchard had signalled a no-ball. Australia could have been tottering on 66 for four, with the real prospect of an extraordinary upset. To the fury of the baying Barmy Army, Waugh then clattered the 'hat-trick ball' for four.

Waugh fell to Caddick for 14, the Somerset bowler also getting Langer, but the Australians held their nerve for a five-wicket victory to keep them firmly on course for a first clean-sweep against England since 1920-21. Harmison's over, however, dominated a large chunk of space in the next day's match reports.

"By the second innings in Melbourne you could really see that this kid had something going for him," says Conn. "In that innings, Harmison just stuck it up them, and he really stuck it up Steve Waugh. Waugh came in late after suffering a migraine and I reckon Harmison had him out three times before he went. That was when people began to sit up."

Waugh accepted that his let-offs had probably been the turning point, adding: "If that wasn't a no-ball, England may well have gone on to win that match."

For England, it was an indication of things to come. "It was the first sign of what we had been expecting and hoping for from him," recalls Hussain. "It was the first sign of what we would see again in 2004. When you consider that spell, you can see why you give Harmy that extra chance to prove himself. It was the last day and the wicket had got pretty slow but we knew he could bowl like that. When you get a batsman of Steve Waugh's class hopping about, you know it's serious. And it wasn't just Waugh who he hurried up that day either."

Against all the odds, England saved face further by winning the last Test in Sydney. Australia, without Warne and McGrath, suddenly looked much less threatening.

Waugh, his Test place under threat, farmed the ecstatic applause of his home supporters by completing a century on the final ball of the second day, equalling Don Bradman's 29 Test centuries while also becoming only the third batsman to score 10,000 Test runs. But, with the game perfectly poised after the first innings, Vaughan again inspired England with an immaculate second knock of 183 to set Australia 452 to win. Harmison even chipped in with 20 not out and an unbeaten 43-run stand with Stewart for the final wicket. Caddick then took the bowling honours. Renowned for being at his best at the least important of times, he cleaned up on the final day with seven for 94 as England won by 225 runs, as well as ending Australia's 22-match unbeaten run at home. Harmison, who took three good wickets in the first innings, added a fourth when dismissing Durham team mate Love for the second time in the match. It was England's first and only victory in a first-class match on tour.

Harmison ended the series with nine wickets at 50.55. Yet he had finished well – he was also credited with bowling a delivery at 94mph, the fastest recorded by an Englishman – and gone a long way to challenge, if not conquer, his personal demons. Arguably those demons, indeed, had presented as great a challenge as Messrs Hayden and Langer. As he put it later: "When I went away last winter, the games were important, but the biggest thing was just to try to stay there, to be happy away from home. It was five months away, and I had a kid born in the middle of it. After that, I wouldn't say I can write the homesickness thing off, but I can certainly put it to one side for a bit. I felt I showed my strength of character. After the Sydney Test, I felt as though I had proved to myself and to others that I can play at Test level."

The tour wound up with a one-day series also involving Sri Lanka. England's injury crisis also opened the door for Harmison's selection for the World Cup, although he would not play a single game during the side's wretched campaign in South Africa, which included a boycott of the match against Zimbabwe.

Harmison, given leave to dash home before the World Cup to see his new daughter, was not a huge success in the VB Series in Australia either, but, again, he came through it. He began the tournament well, but then sent down 11 wides, including five in an over, against Australia in a match England lost by just seven runs. He bowled nine more with two no-balls next up against the Sri Lankans, leading to more wisecracks. Victor Chandler, an independent British bookmaker, even offered odds on how many wides he would bowl. "Geoff Boycott famously described a good delivery as a ball that pitches in the 'corridor of uncertainty' but with Steve it's more like a 'motorway of uncertainty'," the firm said on its website. "On current form he'd struggle against an average village side."

England, however, were much more upbeat, while accepting the jury was still out and deliberating. "He has the potential to provide us with something we haven't had for quite a while," said Hussain. "But he also has the potential to look very average, so we have to work with him and continue to support him."

Any criticisms, however, would have been emphatically drowned out by a few pertinent words from Dennis Lillee earlier in the tour. The former Australia fast bowler, now regarded as the world's leading fast bowling coach, said: "There's something there with Harmison. He's very much worth persevering with, because he's got something."

CHAPTER EIGHT

THE TURNING POINT

The year 2003 – or, more accurately, its final four months – provided the turning point in Harmison's career. The Ashes had suggested a growing maturity and fortitude, off the pitch as well as on it, as if he was finally coming to terms with his calling. For all that, he still had everything to prove. He could make you gasp with the occasional searing delivery which spat up and threatened to decapitate any batsman foolish enough to stand his ground. But, more often than not, there were also two or three winces per over at wide and wasted deliveries. He was still only five matches into his Test career, but the selectors, having championed his cause without wavering, were now seeking signs of an upward trend.

Harmison has suggested that the breakthrough came on September 7 and 8, 2003, at The Oval against South Africa. The statistics back him up. For Geoff Cook, though, it was as much a psychological transformation. "I think those 12 months, from the nightmare with the run-up in Perth, were the period where he really developed mentally. He matured."

Fate seemed to be on his side at the start of the year. After his hard labour in Australia, Harmison was offered the perfect opportunity to gorge himself on cheap wickets against a weakened and confused Zimbabwe side. Instead, he found himself continually being upstaged.

At Lord's, in May, James Anderson was the scene-stealer. The young, quietly spoken Lancastrian had leapt into the public consciousness during the World Cup, swinging the ball prodigiously to emerge as England's best bowler. One delivery, which bent improbably late to flatten Yousuf Youhana's stumps at Newlands, lived long in the memory. With Gough still sidelined and Caddick and Flintoff newly crocked, Anderson made his debut in the First Test against Zimbabwe and inscribed his name on the five-wicket honours board at the first attempt, taking five for 73. After a mediocre start he produced a spell of four wickets for five runs in 14 balls to obliterate the lower order, Zimbabwe crashing to 147 all out and being forced to follow on. Harmison, whose one wicket was taken at fly slip, and Anderson had both been awarded six-month England contracts at the start of the summer but there was no doubt who was hogging the limelight.

In the second innings Harmison, bowling at a furious lick and making the batsmen duck and dive, was again overshadowed, this time by a pair of occasional trundlers. Mark Butcher had scored a century to build the foundations for England, then re-appeared with his medium-pacers to help knock over Zimbabwe's straw-strength batting for a second time. He took four for 60 with some neat outswingers while his ally, the friendly paced Anthony McGrath, took three for 16. Nineteen wickets had fallen on the third day, England had won by an innings and 92 runs, and Harmison must have marvelled at the injustice of it all.

The Second Test was tailor-made for him, even if it meant fielding the odd joke at his own expense. The game was to be staged at Durham's ground, the Riverside becoming England's first new Test venue in over a century. This was as much of a home match as a Test could ever get for Harmison. To his credit, he joined in the fun. "I've never hidden the fact that I don't like travelling," he told the press before the game. "But this time I'm only 40 miles from home, so I should be all right."

Still the locals lived in hope rather than expectation. Durham supporters knew him as a fitful bowler who usually promised more than he delivered. His county wickets cost more than 30 runs apiece and he had taken five wickets in an innings only five times in six years. But this time he was playing against under-powered opponents. Andy Flower and Henry Olonga had retired after their anti-Mugabe protests during the World Cup, leaving the side with only one player, Grant Flower, with a Test century to his name.

Harmison would also be leading the attack. With Hoggard bowing to a knee injury, the home bowler, with a mere six caps, was the most experienced English fast bowler on the pitch.

Richard Johnson, however, Hoggard's replacement, was keen to impress. Aged 28, he was a perennial nearly-man, flitting in and out of the squad but never winning selection, his injury-prone body more often than not the cause. Harmison had dreamt of bowling the historic first delivery at Chester-le-Street and causing mayhem. Johnson, though, and the flick of the coin, put paid to that.

Hussain won the toss and opted to bat. England, after an unconvincing start, crept beyond 400. The England captain, to Harmison's disappointment, then threw the ball to Anderson and Johnson. The Somerset seamer, showing the value of pitching the ball up and bowling wicket to wicket, struck with his third and fourth balls without conceding a run, Anderson joined in with two victims of his own and it was 27 for five before Harmison got on for the fifteenth over. By the end, Johnson had the extraordinary figures of six for 33 off 12 overs, leaving Harmison with the slender pickings of the number nine and ten batsmen as the touring side were dismissed for 94.

In the second innings, Anderson took three of the top four. Harmison at least began proceedings by taking the first wicket and he also hoovered up the tail to end with four wickets for 55, his best Test return. One of his throws from the deep also ran out Heath Streak, so it was a five-for of sorts. England won by an innings to settle the series 2-0.

The one-dayers that followed against Zimbabwe and South Africa were to add to the rapidly growing Anderson fan club. He warmed up for the tournament with a wicket first ball at The Oval, followed by a hat-trick against Pakistan. In the triangular event, he headed England's bowling with 11 wickets at 17.63 each as England won the tournament by trouncing the South Africans in the final. Harmison, still regarded as a limited-overs loose cannon, was given one game, in Bristol, and again was upstaged. By the time he got a bowl the Zimbabweans were 51 for seven and heading for defeat. Harmison conceded 11 runs in his first over and 18 off the three that he was permitted.

In the first two Tests against South Africa, the upstaging would be done by a 22-year-old who, by common consent, had just been handed the most poisoned of chalices – the captaincy of a declining team. Graeme Smith, though, did not appear to have a care in the world as he reduced England and most of his own team-mates to onlookers at Edgbaston and Lord's. The youngest skipper in South African Test history, he had arrived in England with a squad close to crisis after a disastrous showing in their home World Cup. Shaun Pollock had been sacked as captain, Allan Donald put out to grass. Jonty Rhodes was also gone while Lance Klusener was threatening legal action over his omission from the tour. The South Africans were still rated the world's second-best side but England were confident of challenging that assumption. It was a confidence that did not survive for long.

Harmison had prepared for the series in near-perfect circumstances, 'The Ashington Express' teaming up with overseas signing Shoaib Akhtar –'The Rawalpindi Express' – to lead Durham's attack against Yorkshire at Chester-le-

Street. The visitors included Gough, White, Sidebottom and the hostile Steve Kirby in their attack, backed up by the batting of New Zealand captain Stephen Fleming and India all-rounder Yuvraj Singh.

"Sadly, Harmy and Shoaib didn't play too much together," says Cook. "But that game against Yorkshire was fantastic, just like a Test match. We ended up winning on the last afternoon. It was cricket of the highest standard." Harmison took five wickets and Shoaib seven before also clouting the winning runs. The Pakistan pace bowler is renowned as something of a limelight-loving, fast-living creature. He and Harmison share pace and not much else. "I don't know if Steve got much from Shoaib, although Shoaib was very keen to help and advise," says Cook with a laugh. "The contrast was massive, you couldn't get two more different characters. What did Steve make of Shoaib? What does anybody make of Shoaib?"

England had been expecting Gough, Caddick and Hoggard to return from injury for the first Test, increasing the competition for places. Gough, however, was the only one to recover and he was selected for the first time in almost two years. He must have soon been wondering whether it had been as worthwhile as Smith, barely visible behind his barn-door of a bat, and the mercurial Herschelle Gibbs amassed 338 for the first wicket on the opening day. Harmison bowled patchily. His one telling contribution was to fracture Trescothick's finger as he attempted to field a ball in the slips.

Smith, whipping the ball off his legs and driving powerfully through the on side, forged his way to 277, the highest Test score by a South African. Vaughan countered with 156. South Africa led by almost 200 after the first innings and Smith then hammered a quickfire 85 in the hope of forcing a result, but the rain, having washed out the second day, got the better of him. Harmison took two for 138 in the match, conceding more than four an over, but he was not alone. England had managed to take just nine wickets in 171 overs, at a cost of 728 runs.

The real drama, however, was reserved for the immediate aftermath of the contest, when a drained and dispirited Hussain unexpectedly stepped down as captain. Vaughan's fresh leadership in the one-day tournament had clearly undermined Hussain's own position with the Test side. "There are some good lads playing under him and the last thing they want is a tired leader," Hussain said. He did not feel he had lost the team's support but added: "It was very difficult for me – my style of captaincy had been about aggression. On my first day back it was very difficult for me to stand up there and do something different from Michael."

Smith thus started the series with a double-century and a captain's scalp. Three days into the Second Test he had banked a further 259 runs, and this time there would be no escape for Vaughan's England. The new skipper's honeymoon ended abruptly as the home team were skittled for 173 and Smith, the fourth man in history to score successive double-centuries, led his side to 682 for six, their highest ever score. England lost by an innings and 92. It would have been worse still but for Flintoff's despairing 142, including 102 in boundaries, on the final day.

Gough listened to the grinding of his knee joints and, with regret, walked gingerly away from the five-day game with 229 Test wickets packed in his 'coffin'.

Duncan Fletcher did not name names but pointed at the bowlers. Harmison, who dropped too short in taking one for 103, and Anderson, who claimed two for 90 compared to Makhaya Ntini's 10 for 220 for South Africa, must have pricked up their ears when Fletcher commented: "There are some youngsters who don't really appreciate bowling six balls in a row in the same area. They have been brought up on wickets where they just bowl and something will happen to the ball. We've got to make sure that their mindset changes".

Nothing much changed for Harmison at Trent Bridge, but it did for England. Vaughan got lucky in winning an important toss and opted to bat first on a pitch which failed to last. England's old guard made full use of their good fortune on the opening two days, Butcher and Hussain scoring gritty centuries. Anderson then chipped his way through South Africa's lower order to take five for 102 and earn England an 83-run first-innings lead. The home side crashed to 118 all out second time around, Pollock taking six wickets, but it did not matter. James Kirtley, making his debut, exploited the increasingly treacherous bounce even more clinically with six for 34 off 16.2 overs and South Africa dissolved to a 70-run defeat.

Kirtley ended with eight for 114, Anderson with seven for 119. Harmison had taken two for 66. In all, he had conceded 307 runs in the series for five wickets.

A calf injury then ruled him out of the next game at Headingley, though there is some doubt about whether he would have been chosen anyway.

The press at the time seemed evenly divided as to whether Harmison fell or was pushed as Martin Bicknell, ten years after his one previous Test appearance, was called up. Graveney termed it a "horses for courses" selection but five days later and South Africa were back in front in the series, thanks mainly to Gary Kirsten. With South Africa tottering on the opening morning, Kirsten dug in and could not be budged until he had made, as he put it, a typically "horrible" century. Kirsten laid the foundations again in the second innings against an increasingly one-dimensional England seam attack. All-rounder Andrew Hall hit a rapid 99 not out to underline the point, Jacques Kallis took six wickets and the game was won in a canter.

Without the rain of the first Test, Smith might have been leading his side to the finale at The Oval on the brink of a comprehensive triumph. As it was, they led 2-1. Smith must nevertheless have been supremely confident of completing South Africa's first series win in England since readmission.

Instead, England escaped from jail and Harmison, at last, helped spring the lock. His efforts also earned him the admiration and allegiance of his new captain. Vaughan needed a win as badly as anyone. He had blamed the Headingley defeat in part on the failure of county cricket to produce young players of quality but the media, singularly unimpressed by what they saw as a cliched excuse, had turned on him. Some newspapers even aired doubts over his strength of personality. Vaughan's credibility as a leader was being scrutinised after a mere three games in charge.

Largely, it was a question of style. Hussain, sidelined from the final Test with a broken toe, had been a street fighter. Vaughan came across as the exact opposite, one of the world's top batsmen but more ready with a grin than a growl. It would take everyone time to acclimatise to the new regime.

Harmison acclimatised and benefited. As a young player, he had needed Hussain's firm guidance to help him through difficult times. Vaughan's more relaxed style, however, provided a closer fit to Harmison's own character. Not that Vaughan was an easy touch. He knew what he wanted. One of his accents would be on physical fitness and that, too, would help the Durham bowler more than he might have at first realised.

Graveney, England's head of selectors, was well aware of the change of mood. "The captains I have worked with have all been different, have all brought something to the party," said Graveney, "but I think Michael Vaughan is the most rounded. He wants his players to be the fittest, but he also wants them to enjoy the moment of playing for their country.

"I think there is a bit more of a relaxed atmosphere which, again, is a help to Steve. I think Vaughan is a key bloke for him. I don't think there is quite the fear element that there has been before."

When England named their side for The Oval, Thorpe was back on the team sheet, after more than a year away. So was Harmison. England knew they would need 20 wickets from their bowlers on a good batting surface to have any chance of squaring the series, but the opening day yielded just four, at a cost of 362 runs. Gibbs scored 183, with 146 coming in boundaries. England's attack, indeed, was so lacking in bite early on that Vaughan had turned to Giles's left-arm spin after just 12 overs.

Throughout the series, the South Africans had majored on winning the toss – Smith won four out of five – and making emphatic starts. They had made 398 for one after the first day at Edgbaston and 412 for two after the second at Lord's. Gibbs's performance, backed up by the unflappable Kirsten, seemed to have settled the series.

England, though, blew on the embers on day two. South Africa's last eight wickets fell for 139, everyone bar Harmison chipping in. Bicknell started things in the first over by removing Jacques Rudolph and the wickets kept falling. Giles provided another key ingredient – luck – by finger-tipping a return drive into the stumps at the non-striker's end to get rid of Kallis.

Trescothick, taking a leaf out of Smith's book, then hammered 219 while Thorpe scored a century and the game was back on. Flintoff, his reputation growing by the day, scored 95 and put on 99 with Harmison, who contributed a studious three runs to the partnership. England, 120 ahead, finally declared one session into the fourth day on 604 for nine.

Bicknell and Harmison then teamed up to set up a famous England victory. The two complemented each other perfectly. Physically, they were similar – both lean, tall men, with

Bicknell claiming half-an-inch in height advantage. They could not have been more different in the way they went about their craft, however. The Surrey man, at 36 Harmison's senior by a dozen years, could have had a career as an English Glenn McGrath if he had only had an extra yard of pace. An old-fashioned English seamer, he concentrated on impeccable line and length coupled by swing and seam movement, while his partner concentrated on out-and-out pace and vicious bounce. Merge the two and you might produce the perfect bowler. Vaughan, however, was just glad to have the pair in tandem at The Oval as they took four wickets each. Harmison rooted out Kirsten and Kallis from the top order in consecutive overs, the pivotal moments of the fourth afternoon, as he bowled 13 overs for 25 runs either side of tea. He returned on the final morning to add Pollock and Ntini in a second spell of 6.2-3-10-2 to finish with his best figures for England, four for 33 off 19.2 overs. Bicknell, meanwhile, twitching the ball both ways, accounted for Smith, Rudolph, Boucher and Hall in taking four for 84 off 24.

A packed fifth-day crowd saw England rattle off the 110 required for a nine-wicket win while Stewart, in his last Test, looked on from the pavilion. England, in tabloid speak, had gone from dunces to diamond geezers in a matter of days.

Vaughan could barely believe the turnaround himself. "Throughout my short career to date this is my best Test victory," he said. "Steve Harmison was fantastic and Martin Bicknell, on his home ground, was exceptional."

Bicknell enjoyed his twilight fairytale but it was to be the end of such adventures for him. England would not call again. For Harmison, though, it was just the start of an extraordinary 12 months.

CHAPTER NINE

FROM HORSE TO TROY

Look back on anyone's life and you will stumble over a complex network of 'what ifs'. What if, standing at that junction, he had turned left instead of right, or pushed on instead of retracing his steps?

Harmison's road has been no different. Where would he be today if Durham had not gained first-class status? What would have happened if Cook, Gifford and Boon had not been so sympathetically committed to his cause? What if Harmison himself had decided, after his wretched first foray to Pakistan, that he preferred a quieter, more parochial life? What would have transpired had he decided that he lacked the resolve to tackle his fears head on?

Troy Cooley is another Harmison 'what if'. For many, indeed, he would become the most prominent 'what if' of them all. What if Cooley had stayed at home in Australia, or severed his ties with the game after an unsuccessful playing career?

"There are so many elements but I'm convinced the biggest influence on Harmison's career has been Troy," says Graveney. It seems likely that, without Cooley's input as England bowling coach, Harmison's career would have stalled long before he built up enough speed for take-off.

Like Boon, Cooley hails from Launceston, a Tasmanian city of around 100,000 people. His early career as a cricketer shared eerie similarities with that of his future charge. As a youngster in the mid 1980s, he bowled seriously fast, cutting swathes through opposing batting line-ups in club cricket but, like Harmison, he was burdened with an imperfect technique. He watched and revered Lillee, as well as Michael Holding, who played a season for the state side. Attempting to impress, he would have hurled thunderbolts down at Boon and the likes of Ponting in the nets. Unlike Harmison, he dreamt of becoming a professional cricketer.

He only managed 33 first-class games for Tasmania, however. Once, he played against a touring England side. But while club cricketers had trembled before him, better class players did not. Cooley could still frighten, but dismissing batsmen at the higher level was another matter. In all, he took 54 wickets at 61.35 apiece. Injuries did not help but he struggled with no-balls in particular. He never solved the problem and nor did his coaches. Pace without control was simply not enough. After a ten-year career with more stops than starts, he called it a day in 1995, a year before Harmison would come to Durham's notice.

A fitness enthusiast, Cooley turned to running a gym, which many of his former colleagues frequented. That helped him retain his close links with the game. A few years later, Tasmania asked him back to help out with their fast bowlers. In those days, coaches often relied on directives rather than discussion and explanation. Sometimes more hearsay was involved than science. Cooley, though, became increasingly interested in the bio-mechanics of the bowling action, stripping things back to the fundamentals and making it easier to explain to bowlers why one approach might work and another not.

He found that his growing knowledge made sense of bowling and that, as a result, players listened. His experience of gym work also made him understand that tailored work-outs, rather than general muscle-building, could play a key part in injury prevention and bowling prowess. His former hero, Lillee, had moved into elite coaching and Cooley followed in his mentor's footsteps, eventually working at Australia's Cricket Academy.

It was there that he first came across England's new crop of quicks. Rod Marsh had been recruited to build England their own Academy in an attempt to bridge the divide between county and Test cricket, and he sought out the best help he could find. With the England Academy temporarily basing itself Down Under while it waited for a permanent home, some of the best expertise available was right on the doorstep. "Troy would have been used at that time by Rod, just as he uses a number of specialised coaches, like Ashley Mallett, Dennis Lillee and Ian Chappell," says Graveney.

Marsh had left Australia for England in search of a new challenge and Cooley would do the same. Everything was running smoothly in Adelaide. In England, the building blocks needed to be put in place. And the raw material offered by Harmison, Flintoff and Jones, big strong young men with high actions, must have been hugely enticing.

Cooley applied for the post of England's National Academy Fast Bowling Coach in 2003 and, with Marsh's approval, was appointed in April, just before Zimbabwe arrived on tour. The position also gave him responsibilities for youth and women players as well as county bowlers. Crucially, he would also be seconded to work with England's national side following the departure of Graham Dilley.

Cooley had already won Harmison's trust and respect when the pair had worked together in Australia. Cooley had also tendered advice when approached during the Ashes tour. Harmison was delighted with the appointment and the prospect of a closer collaboration. It would soon pay dividends.

"To say that I was happy when Troy got the job would be an understatement," he told Geoffrey Dean of *The Times*. "I felt I could trust him when I first met him at The Academy in Adelaide, where he was excellent when I asked him a few things. If he wasn't England bowling coach, I'd still be ringing him up."

Cooley took little time to see what needed tweaking. Harmison's arms – "long levers," Cooley calls them – used to swing left and right across his body as he ran in, causing him to sway sideways. He had a huge, ragged jump at the crease and was not strong enough to stop his pelvis tilting as he crash-landed into his delivery stride. He also failed to cock his wrist properly, so that the ball often sprayed off line. Those imperfections, however, did not mask his natural attributes.

"I definitely saw he had something special," said Cooley. "He is six feet four inches tall and, when you add the length of his arm, the ball is coming down from out of the clouds. He had a bit of a balance problem, and at his size you need to be stable. But he was getting it right occasionally."

Cooley also realised that Harmison was not physically strong enough to support his own style of fast bowling. His core muscles and legs needed to be strengthened dramatically.

"It was a key issue. Without that, he couldn't hold the rest of the changes we wanted to drip-feed into him. If you are not stable through the crease, and instead you are fighting left and right rather than taking the momentum to the target, you are not going to get a good bowling position."

That would take time. When Cooley began work in England, the national side were already going into battle against Zimbabwe, with South Africa to arrive a month later. Technical tweaks, like getting Harmison to run with his arms pumping back and forwards in line with his run-up rather than swinging sideways, could be suggested and gradually introduced, but the physical transformation required would have to wait for a significant break in the playing schedule.

It cannot be coincidence, however, that Harmison's sudden

development from sporadic to spectacular coincided almost exactly with Cooley's arrival.

Graveney has no doubts. "There's lots of good coaches but there are some that are outstanding and Rod's philosophy has always been to get the very best, if it can be afforded," he says. "And Troy is the best. Anybody who works under Dennis Lillee has got to be a pretty good bowling coach.

"In fact, he's outstanding. That's not just a view held by people within the England set-up. He goes around the counties talking to county bowlers. He's been an outstanding addition to the English game.

"He improved Harmy's action as he has done with pretty much every bowler he has worked with. The bio-mechanics of bowling are pretty logical. Now, with modern equipment, you can analyse every single delivery. Before, you just had to second-guess if it was the right action or not. It's not just his technical knowledge but also the way he goes about his work. It's one thing having the knowledge but it's another to impart it and get the guys to understand it."

Hussain, too, believes that Cooley has succeeded on two fronts with Harmison.

"It's a mixture," he said. "There were technical things that Harmy needed to do. Personally I was always happy when he was bowling at 89-90 miles an hour. I was a bit worried when he started getting up to 94 or 95. I thought he would lose his action. I still think he bowls a little short as well. Even now, I think he could be a lot fuller than he is.

"At Lilac Hill during the 2002-3 Ashes they were all leg-side wides – it was all to do with his wrist position. Troy has managed to help him adjust his wrist and his run-up – that's the technical side. But it's man management again. The bowlers love Troy. He gets the balance right – being strong with them as well as being their mate.

"Graham Dilley was too much their mate – everything was

a beer and a fag. He was a shoulder to cry on. If I had handed out a bollocking and said 'Come on, we need more balls in the business area,' I didn't want the bowling coach to say: 'Don't worry about it, it's the batsmen's fault for not getting enough runs.' Then the guy would go to bed thinking he had done nothing wrong. I wanted somebody to reinforce what I was saying.

"Troy has always been good with the bowlers. He is one of them but, when a kick is needed, he gives them a kick."

Harmison put it like this. "Troy speaks common sense. He speaks to you properly and doesn't try to baffle you with science or cricketing terms," he said. "The thing is, he's a good bloke, and if somebody is a good bloke there is more likelihood that you'll listen."

Study film of Harmison pre-Cooley and post-Cooley and the contrast is telling. The coach often says he did little more than tweak, but the bowler's rocking to left and right has been replaced by a more lithe, athletic and stable run-up. That has fed into a more consistent leap into delivery, with a controlled double-arm gather. Stewart, standing behind the stumps, saw the changes kick in at first hand.

"I've never bowled but the keeper is in a great position to see things," he says. "Bowlers and keeper normally have a great relationship. You can go up and say: 'Your wrist is in the wrong position', or 'Your leading arm is going out to extra cover.' The biggest thing is that he's now working in straight lines. Everything needs to be coming down the wicket. He always jumped up but he would never do it straight and follow through straight. He was inconsistent. There will still be moments when he falls back, but he has improved out of sight."

There seems a certain irony that the man who helped kick-start Harmison's career failed as a player himself because there was no comparable expertise to call upon in his day.

Cooley, however, is loath to look beyond Harmison himself when trying to pinpoint the definitive cause of his success. He also avoids comparing the bowler with others who have gone before.

"Who does he remind me of? Stephen Harmison. He's unique. I'm a great believer that the cream rises to the top. Without the knowledge we can give him, Steve may still have found another way to make it.

"Today, you have some pretty good bio-mechanical evidence to show players. In the old days, they just told you to stop doing things without explaining why they were happening. Now we can explain, so it is easier for players to buy into it. But they take the responsibility to get organised. The success is down to Stephen."

The statistics, though, best underline one man's influence on another.

Midway through the series against South Africa, the Durham bowler had played in nine Tests, taking six wickets at just over 37 each. He had yet to take five wickets in an innings and had not yet influenced a game enough to be made man of the match. In the next year, he would play 14 Tests, taking 76 wickets at 20.51 runs apiece and take five wickets on four occasions. He also won four man-of-the-match awards as well as two for man of the series. It is an extraordinary turnaround, and one in which Cooley's "common sense" clearly played a part.

Harmison, once coached by a man called 'Horse'– Geoff Arnold – before linking up with Troy, was to suffer a dramatic relapse in 2005 on the return tour to South Africa.

Several contributing factors have been offered as explanations, none of which can be proved without doubt. The fact that Cooley only remained with the squad for the first three matches before returning to his National Academy work was one of the more popular theories put forward.

CHAPTER TEN

SO WHAT DO YOU WANT OUT OF LIFE?

Harmison walked away from the South Africa series feeling as if he had made his mark. For a couple of days, the press would be good, with Botham lauding him as the future of English fast bowling. But that warm glow of success did not last long.

England announced their squad for the tours to Bangladesh and Sri Lanka and Harmison was selected. He had not been sure of being picked, considering the slow-low wickets of Asia, but his performance at The Oval made him impossible to ignore. Soon after, however, the squad's central contracts were announced and Harmison's name was not on the list.

He took it as a slight. He had played in 11 of England's previous 12 Tests, more than any other bowler. Still raw, he had contributed to the few English high points of the 2002-2003 Ashes, ruffled the Zimbabweans and then helped the team to fight back from the brink to hold the South Africans. While Harmison had been overlooked, his good friend and county team-mate Paul Collingwood had been awarded a 12-month deal, even though he had yet to win his first Test cap. "I'm stunned, to be honest," Harmison told the *Newcastle Chronicle.* "The only thing I can think of is that the contracts were decided before the Oval game." He talked with Graveney but remained dissatisfied with what he was told. Not everyone, though, agreed with him.

Michael Henderson, writing for the *Wisden Cricketer,* pointed out that, despite his grand finale, Harmison had taken an underwhelming nine wickets at 45 runs apiece against South Africa and suggested that a little less talking and a bit more wicket-taking, starting in Dhaka, might be in order. The selectors, it said, had stuck by him through the thin times and it was now his turn to repay them.

Others interpreted the decision as a Fletcher ploy to galvanise the languid Harmison into showing more commitment to his fitness work. They read it as a reminder that he was employed under England's terms, not his own.

More questions over the bowler's determination to exploit his talent might have resurfaced soon after, had the details of a players' private chat just before the tour of Bangladesh leaked out. The England squad had assembled early in October on the day before the flight out and several players congregated for a drink. "I remember we were in a bar or a hotel, about to fly off to Bangladesh the next morning," recalls Hussain. "We were having a discussion and everyone was asking me how long I was going to go on playing. There was me, Butch, Vaughan, Gilo and Harmy, having a few rum and cokes. Harmy, after a few of whatever he was drinking, said: 'Well, give me a few years and I might be off. Give me three or four years and that will do me.' You could see the captain's eyes open up wide, you could almost hear him thinking: 'What? Look, we've got a lot of investment in you!' "

Harmison's comments, to some, might have betrayed a lack of commitment to the collective cause. His critics would surely have condemned him for taking the money and running. Hussain, though, was neither surprised, shocked nor particularly concerned.

"You could see that all the way through his career. It's almost a take-it-or-leave-it with him. With me, that was never an option. It was always take it. For him, the attitude was: 'I don't necessarily need this.' "

He also saw it as an example of Harmison's no-nonsense honesty.

"That's Harmy for you," said Hussain. "He's not one to sit there and think: 'The captain's next to me and Nasser's opposite me, I'd better say the right things, what they want to hear.' I know people like that, who know what they want to do, deep down, but say the opposite.

"Anyway, there are ways of handling him so that those three or four years become five or six, or seven or eight. You don't know. Things change. He may feel differently in three or four years. You don't want him saying that, of course, but he speaks honestly and you just have to look after him."

It was Harmison who looked after England in the inaugural Test against Bangladesh. By then, Anderson and Flintoff had both been ruled out of the series with injury, leaving the team to rely on the thinnest of new-ball attacks, with Harmison at one end and Hoggard, who had just regained fitness, at the other. The Bangladeshis, with 23 defeats and one weather-induced draw out of 24 Tests, were supposed to be a push-over. But they had just run Pakistan close in one match, the home team requiring an unbeaten century by Inzamam-ul-Haq to win by a single wicket.

Rain curtailed the first day of the First Test in Dhaka to 15 overs, by which time Harmison, mixing up fuller deliveries, seamers and rib-cage balls, had taken two for nine off seven overs. The next day, he opened with another six-over spell, claiming his third wicket in the process, then returned at the death with the final two wickets in two overs as the home side were dismissed for 203. Harmison had taken five wickets for the first time, for 35 runs off 21.5 overs and on a pitch expected to neuter him. The only criticism was that he had bowled a shade too wide of off-stump.

England, despite a Trescothick century, managed only a 92-run lead and when Bangladesh reached 120 for one in their second innings early on the fourth day, an upset looked possible. The next nine wickets, though, only added a further 135 as Harmison and Hoggard, with little effective support from the spinners in the hot and humid conditions, kept rumbling in without protest. Hoggard took seven wickets in the match as England wrapped up a comfortable victory. Harmison took four for 44 off 25 overs in the second innings and was named man of the match for his nine for 79. In all, he had bowled a monumental 46.5 overs. His performance had come against cricketing minnows but those who witnessed it were impressed with his increasing accuracy and consistency.

Again, though, bad news rapidly followed good. By the time the team flew into Chittagong, Harmison's back had stiffened up. Back problems are notoriously difficult to diagnose and it was decided to fly him home for checks before his return for the Sri Lanka leg of the tour. Johnson replaced him in the Second Test against Bangladesh and, in a near-duplicate performance, took nine wickets and the man-of-the-match award.

Whispers soon circulated that Harmison had not put up a fight when it was suggested to him that he should head back to England. Those whispers would redouble when Harmison failed to rejoin the touring squad. All seemed to be going well, early in November, when the England and Wales Cricket Board announced that a series of back scans revealed no significant damage. Dr Peter Gregory, England's chief medical officer, said there would be more treatment and strengthening work and that he was "very optimistic" that the player would be ready in a month's time for Sri Lanka. Within two weeks, however, Harmison had been ruled out of the tour after failing a fitness test at the National Academy.

Some reports referred to Harmison's "mystery" back problem while a few senior players out in Sri Lanka fanned the flames with off-the-record remarks to journalists, making clear their displeasure. Hussain says the speculation was inevitable.

"The problem is that when you get a reputation, it seems impossible to shake it off. It was the same with me. I had a reputation for being a bad boy. Steve has got a reputation for wanting to go home, so every time he goes home everyone is going to question it," he said.

"The fact that it was also Bangladesh didn't help. It's not an easy place to tour and it's a long way away. So people thought he didn't want to be there.

"Touring sometimes is like being at school or like being among a group of tetchy old women. Everyone starts chatting and some start bickering. 'We're staying out here and Harmy is going home. Typical Harmy, he doesn't want to do the work.' But fast bowlers do get injured.

"It's a question of team spirit. I see this stuff on television, with the huddles. It's all very well but that is not team spirit. Team spirit is when someone like Steve Harmison does what he did and, because he's been there for you and backed you up in team meetings and stuff, you have to back him up. Unless you know 100 per cent that he's skiving, you have to go around and say: 'We accept he's gone home, he'll be back in the fold, he's an asset and we need him.'"

Not everyone in Sri Lanka was so forgiving, as England's tour gradually stalled. They were crushed by 10 wickets in the first one-day international after being dismissed for 88, their second lowest score in history. Rain washed out the next two matches.

With the irrepressible Flintoff and Giles trying to hold the attack together, England's batsmen then fought two long rearguard actions to save the first two Tests only to run out of steam after an arduous trip and fail in Colombo. They were thumped by an innings and 215 runs, Sri Lanka's largest margin of victory ever and England's third heaviest defeat.

As this unfolded, Harmison, back in England, was unhappy about his rehabilitation work. He did not want to stay at Loughborough to carry it out, but was also disgruntled with the alternative – long car trips from Ashington, several times a week – and asked if he could train nearer to home. It made sense but was translated into suggestions that he was unwilling to put the hard graft in. There were whispers, both in the media and expressed among the players, that his lack of drive might lead to him being left out of the tour to the West Indies in March.

Harmison hit back with an article in the *Daily Mirror*, underlining his commitment to play for England and branding the criticism as rubbish. "Even the old chestnut about my homesickness has come up again, and that is bitterly disappointing because I thought we had nailed that once and for all last winter," he said. "Sure, the first couple of weeks in Bangladesh were hard and at times the homesickness thing did kick in, but I still knuckled down and took nine wickets in Dhaka on a dead pitch."

His complaints about his rehabilitation he put down to "a difference of opinion" with the selectors, adding he had been bitterly disappointed to come home from Bangladesh and would be just as disappointed not to tour the West Indies.

Things came to a head with a meeting between the player and the selectors at Loughborough. In later interviews, Harmison recalled that his agent, John Morris, had called for the meeting. "There was flak flying round in the press," he told Simon Wilde of *The Sunday Times* "I wanted some answers as to where this whispering campaign came from. John said to them, 'I want this sorted out. I want you lot to say what the **** is going on.' They said, 'We're not sure where it's come from'. They weren't happy with me and I wasn't happy with them, but everything got sorted out in the end. Basically, they said 'We're sticking by you. Get yourself fit, you go to the West Indies.' "

"It reassured me. I wasn't sure they were batting on my team. When I walked out of that meeting, I knew they did want me."

Graveney says it was not a heated affair, and it did help to clear the air. "There had been some statements which originated from Bangladesh and there was some adverse press comment, over which John Morris probably wanted some clarification. That was probably the reason why Morris wanted to come and see what was going on," says Graveney.

"We were down at Loughborough on other business anyway, so we took the opportunity to have a chat to Harmy, since he was down there doing his rehab. We asked him about the tour, how he felt things were going, what he wanted out of life. It was a confidential conversation but it wasn't heavy duty, I have to say.

"But he did need to get much fitter. I think he suddenly realised he was getting increasingly frustrated with the continual chain of injury and really started to embrace fitness. History shows what happened next. The Loughborough regime is a wake-up call for anybody. I think that would have got through to him, that he could get greater success by staying fit.

"The modern cricketer knows that, financially, a career playing for England can set you up for life. I think that point would have been made by John Morris. I'm sure it would have been pointed out to Harmison by his friends – that he and his family could have everything that they wanted. His natural talent was enormous, so it was logical for him to get himself fit and play.

"Duncan Fletcher was very keen on Harmison and felt he was key for the West Indies, as long as he was fit. It was an important time for his rehab. It was a case of saying: 'Don't forget your mates are away in pretty tough conditions playing on flat wickets, so rehab means rehab'. I don't think there was any worry that he did not want to succeed, I think he was just a bit confused, depressed about a bit of success being followed by injury all the time. That can wear you down. From then on, though, he just reinvented himself."

The meeting paved the way to an agreement that Harmison should be allowed to continue his rehabilitation nearer to home, and it did not take long to find the perfect place.

CHAPTER ELEVEN

IN A NEWCASTLE SHIRT AT LAST

Shortly after Bangladesh, a story began to do the rounds. One of England's best cricketing prospects, fresh from having his attitude surreptitiously questioned, had made the bizarre decision to go and train at his local Premier League football club. The sceptics probably felt he had taken the opportunity to spend some time chatting to his Newcastle United idols. For others, it provided the perfect tabloid tale. Inspired by Newcastle manager Sir Bobby Robson, Steve Harmison was slogging around the pitch at St James' Park next to his boyhood hero Alan Shearer, playing five-a-side matches and impressing everyone with his footballing skills. Neither of those versions came close to the truth.

Paul Winsper – a man with a name less suited to attractive headlines than Robson and Shearer – positively crackles with enthusiasm. It comes off him in waves. He looks you right in the eye and speaks fast and fluently, his words driven on by a passion for his work. Of no more than average height, he looks young, nimble and lean as he enters his 40s. His short cropped hair, like his bearing, spells military.

Get Newcastle United's conditioning coach to speak about Steve Harmison and he rattles along without pausing for breath. Get to know him better, and Winsper might let you know that he owns a special piece of cricketing memorabilia – one of the two shirts that the Durham bowler wore when taking his historic seven-wicket haul against West Indies.

If Cooley was the man who inspired Harmison by translating complex bio-mechanical theory into everyday English, then it was Winsper who helped make sure that the young man's frame would be robust enough to transform that theory into reality. If Cooley crossed the Ts, then Winsper helped dot the Is. He proved to be the right man in the right place at exactly the right time, according to Durham's director of cricket, Geoff Cook.

"He knew Harmy already," he says. "And Paul's a top man. It was probably the perfect time in Stephen's development. England had put a massive onus on fitness for a while. Some people accept it, some don't as much, that's human nature. But Stephen realised that to get where he wanted to be, he would have to do something about it. Paul's approach was very scientific and it was convenient, being so local. And it was at Newcastle United. So there were lots of good things about it."

Winsper would not have appeared as a likely ally a few years before. For a start, cricket was not his game. A more than useful footballer in his early years, he became an accomplished tri-athlete before snapping a cruciate ligament. At school, he had done well academically and been offered a university place but, keen to stay closer to home, he had opted instead for a job as an insurance underwriter. "I hated it," he says.

He kept himself smiling by joining the Royal Marines reserves, ploughing through Norwegian snowdrifts and scaling Scottish mountains. He thrived on the challenge but ultimately decided against an army career. A new job as a pension adviser promised a good salary and a company car but, aged 27, his wife told him it was time to stop pretending. She would bring in the money while he went back to university to study what he now recognised had become his passion.

Winsper graduated with a first-class degree in sport and exercise science from Northumbria University. Then, having been offered lecturing work, he began studying for a masters (circumstances meant he was never able to complete it) while joining a Sports Council-funded initiative part-time to set up an academy for young players at Durham County Cricket Club.

"Geoff and I sat down and worked the programme out," he says. "We wanted to give the kids a physical, nutritional, psychological and injury prevention grounding." Cook provided the cricket expertise while Winsper concentrated on the physical side. Experts were drafted in when needed. One of the top physiotherapists in the country was hired to screen the players. A British Olympic sports psychologist trained the players in concentration, visualisation and goal-setting. Nutritionists advised them on what to eat and when.

If Harmison had not been so meteoric a success at Durham, he might have learnt to give up his beloved burgers and chips and train more assiduously as a teenager. He might, indeed, have learnt methods to try to tackle his homesickness. But his rapid promotion from teenage discovery to the first XI meant that he leapfrogged the academy straight into the Durham front line.

"He would come into the gym and do bits and pieces," says Winsper. "We always got on very well, but he was never the best in the gym or on the runs. It was very different with Steve, it was a matter of cajoling him into it –'Let's try this again. What about that?'

"He was the kind of person who loved to play cricket or football. But lying down to do stretches for the sake of stretching... well, why? That is fine, because it showed his single-minded determination. He never once said to me, 'I'm not doing it.' But he didn't really embrace it, or take it on board. I suppose I was also a bit naïve then. We wanted to

144

work people hard and strengthen them mentally. I was fresh from university, and I thought I could change the world."

Aged 19, Harmison possessed an undeveloped, stick-insect physique paired with the begrudging manner of an ill-at-ease teenager. Winsper concedes he had to have the young man's potential explained to him.

"I couldn't just watch a cricketer and say he was going to be world class. I just listened to Geoff and Norman. He had hit a growth spurt. His co-ordination was poor, and he couldn't control the very little strength that he had. His legs and arms used to go all over the place. But they were all saying he bowled from his full height, he didn't fall away. If we could harness that, then we would have a top international bowler. These were Geoff's exact words: 'If we get it right, we've got a top bowler here.'"

Cook had just enticed Harmison back to the club after his fateful tour of Pakistan with the England Under-19s and was keen to speed up his progress. Winsper realised that Harmison would require a specialised programme – "he couldn't just go and do six-mile runs, because his back tightened, his hamstrings would go and he'd get shin splints" – but by mid-1997 Winsper had been poached by Newcastle United football club.

A short time later, Winsper got a call from Cook to ask whether Harmison could visit the Newcastle United Academy to help with his general fitness. Winsper said yes, but it didn't quite work.

"I was trying to establish myself at Newcastle. I had other commitments and Stephen was doing other things. I couldn't give him the one-on-one that he needed. He was joining in group strength sessions, but he needed something very different."

Coach and player thus headed off in different directions after little more than a brief acquaintance. Harmison, injuries notwithstanding, gradually made a name for himself at Durham while Winsper did the same at Newcastle. Their paths would not cross professionally for around six years.

Contact was re-established via a fortuitous and circuitous route. Newcastle United goalkeeping coach Simon Smith was a good friend of Paul Farbrace, a coach at England's National Cricket Academy. That link led to a group of cricket coaches visiting St James' Park on a fact-finding mission. Winsper was addressing his audience on the need for detailed, personalised training programmes, arguing that cricketers would not benefit from arduous yomps and bench-press sessions, when the name of Harmison cropped up. Back from Bangladesh, he was trekking down from Ashington to Loughborough – several hours each way, a couple of times a week and with a permanent scowl etched on his face – in an attempt to get fit. Would it be possible, Winsper was asked, for him to use the nearby Newcastle United facilities instead?

Winsper found himself excited by the idea. His previous links with Harmison made it easy to say yes. Bobby Robson's love of cricket meant the club had no objections. Durham, too, were happy. The state-of-the-art gym at the club's training centre in Benton, just to the north of the city, was used every day by around 60 football players. An extra body would make little difference. The only significant demands would be on Winsper's time and, more importantly, on Harmison's commitment.

Outwardly, he may have appeared as nonchalant as ever but the 24-year-old had a point to prove, both to himself and certainly to his detractors. He knew he was being offered a perfect opportunity, and at his spiritual sporting home.

"I knew he wanted it desperately and I knew that he was committed to it this time," says Winsper. "I was more than happy to help."

It was January 2004, nine weeks before the start of the West Indies tour. The early physical tests were not encouraging as Harmison, towering over most of the Newcastle players around him but with less than half the muscle mass, loped into the gym. Winsper, used to working with finely tuned athletes, realised he had a job on his hands.

"He wasn't injured but he wasn't what I would call fit. He was certainly nowhere near fit to bowl at top speed. I'm not sure he had ever been," Winsper says. Harmison, basically, was under-powered and not strong enough to hold his bowling action together. But he did have natural stamina, a legacy of his teenage years of playing sport at every opportunity. "I would have had a problem if his endurance base had been very bad, because I would have had to build that up before starting the strength work, but it wasn't. His strength was the problem.

"We basically had to take him all the way back to basics to rebuild him to where he needed to be for the West Indies. I had him coming in up to six days a week, from around nine in the morning to three in the afternoon. On his day off, he went to watch Newcastle United.

"I knew that if we could work systematically, nine weeks would be enough."

They began with what Winsper terms a "basic functional movement assessment". The coach looked at Harmison's knees, the flexibility of his ankles, the strength of his muscles and whether he could stabilise "what we call the core of the body." Winsper added: "I found so many deficiencies."

Harmison had mentioned Cooley's innovative approach and the two coaches decided on an early meeting. Cooley journeyed north armed with his laptop and video clips of Harmison's bowling action. "I had never heard of Troy before Steve mentioned him," says Winsper.

"Without a doubt I wanted to hear his ideas. I'm no expert.

The Durham players will tell you that. I'm a very poor cricketer. Once, on a pre-season tour to Sussex, I had worked the players really hard and then made them dive off the pier and swim back to the beach. They got back for a net session that afternoon, padded me up and forced me in the nets. The fast bowlers sent down spin and the spinners were bowling pace but I still didn't see anything."

Cooley and Winsper formed an immediate bond. "He really knows his stuff and he's very refreshing because he keeps things simple. It's all about straight lines, rather than overcomplicating everything," says Winsper. "He showed me all the movements and said this was what we needed, bio-mechanically, for Stephen's bowling action. I basically worked the conditioning programme back from that ideal action."

Harmison's previous gym work had been traditional in character, working out on the sort of machines seen in most gyms. "That approach has a good, solid effect," says Winsper, "but in making you stronger, such work does not rectify underlying problems." Now the bowler found himself leaping off a machine with elastic straps pulling him back to the ground while Winsper looked on. "When I put him on those pieces of equipment I realised, as his foot landed, everything was falling away. He didn't have the strength in his hips or the core of the body to hold it together. It was kind of collapsing. So when he bowled he was trying to compensate by driving through with his shoulder, and this was causing pains in his shins.

"The first priority is always injury prevention. There is no point in having huge amounts of power if you are always injured. Once you are happy that the muscles are strong enough and stable enough to carry out the movements, then you move on to the power. But he wasn't coming in to do power exercises. There wasn't really time for that. He was coming in to do very boring, methodical strengthening exercises."

A series of specifically designed drills were devised. "He thought I was crazy half of the time but he did them," he said. Harmison found himself hopping up and down, then crouching one-legged to collect a rolling medicine ball before flinging it away, hopping up again and powering off into a short sprint. Every day he worked on a large inflatable ball, doing a string of exercises and weight sessions that worked the wall of muscle around his pelvis. In the beginning he couldn't even sit on the ball without tumbling off, let alone exercise on it. Then he was put into a machine that made him pull cables down and across his torso, working all the rotational muscles in his shoulders and sides.

"He remarked that what we were doing was very different from what he had done before. It was a big motivation for Stephen that he saw the Newcastle players doing similar things."

The results were assessed, routines tweaked and then repeated ad nauseam. Winsper prefers the word "methodical", adding: "He was generally weak. He needed building up.

"The fitness work provides the base to start bowling. Players do get fit to bowl by bowling, but they require a strong conditioning foundation from which to start. The basic preparation allows your body to handle the stresses. I just said to Stephen that we were training in order to train."

Where once Harmison had shown a marked antipathy towards work, Winsper now found he would comply as long as each exercise was explained to him. "It was fantastic, a breath of fresh air. He would come in and say: 'Let's do it.' We sat down, I explained everything. Was he excited? He's not really a very excitable chap, is he? That's Harmy. Takes it all in his stride. It's his style. He just gets on with it. As long as I kept him in the loop and explained why, he didn't have a problem."

The drills were rotated to avoid muscle fatigue and reduce the risk of injury. There was also some endurance work but bench presses – "what exactly does a bowler need biceps for?" – barely featured. "He did some light work on his upper body, but it wasn't a body builder's programme. I didn't care what he looked like," says Winsper. "I was worried how functionally he could move."

Occasionally, as a reward and to vary the routine, Harmison took part in sessions with the Newcastle players around him. "Sometimes players like Gary Speed, Aaron Hughes and Jermaine Jenas might be doing a similar programme, so I suppose I gave him a bit of a treat. But he was not star-struck. The press said he was going around star-struck, it was not like that at all. He came in and got on with things. The lads took to him. They all chatted, asking him about his sport and pulling his leg by saying cricketers were all soft and had things easy.

"Our players are in the gym most days, including Alan (Shearer). Everybody is at work, but there is always friendly banter during recovery periods. One of our goalkeepers, Steve Harper, was a very good cricketer, and he and Robbie Elliott were among those who took a real interest in Harmy's career. Harper took a big liking to Harmy. He knew who Stephen was and what he was capable of. The banter and camaraderie that built up was fantastic.

"Harmy knew all the players by name, of course, and generally the squad knew who Harmy was. Some of them didn't have a clue – our French players were wondering who this giant was in the gym – but they were fine with him. And when the cricket came on TV later, they had a little look."

Eventually, it leaked out that Harmison was training at Newcastle and the press picked up on the story. Winsper and his charge had agreed not to talk about it in public, in an attempt to avoid criticism if the training proved less successful than hoped. The press coverage, however, was largely speculative and the club decided that Winsper should give a round of interviews to clarify the situation.

"Not once did he run around kicking a football," he said. "People were saying he was playing five-a-side with Alan Shearer and taking shots at Shay Given. The club said I would have to put that to bed, so I did a piece saying it was conditioning work only, in the gym."

The effort soon began to pay off. Harmison was benefiting in particular from the one-to-one attention and a fresh perspective. Winsper said: "Sometimes I overlook things with our Newcastle players. Bang! You're in the gym with 24 players, it's mayhem, and the priority is safety so that they don't drop a weight on their foot. It kind of washes over and suddenly the session is finished, whereas with Harmy I was able to work much more closely. With my background with Durham, I understood the demands of cricket but I was outside the cricket loop. I was able to take a very objective stance. This is the man, this is what he has to do. How am I going to get him to do that without him breaking down? That was the basic issue."

Nine methodical weeks later Winsper knew that Harmison was ready. "I was absolutely delighted. I did the same functional movement screening just before he left and it was incredible. Even the players were commenting on the change. That was down to his determination, to every day thinking: 'It's not going to beat me, I'm going to do it.'"

When Harmison finished his final session, Robson – "he was fantastic throughout, as was the chairman Freddy Shepherd and the whole club" – made an appearance to wish him all the best. Winsper was almost sad to see him go.

"If I had to sum it up, I would say I probably enjoyed that

time more than he did. It was a time when our players were competing in Europe and travelling all over the place and it was nice to come back and do something different rather than just recovery sessions.

"It was fantastic to start Steve almost from scratch and build him up. It was brilliant to say: 'This is where he is and that is where I want him to be and that's how long we've got and that's how we are going to get him there'. And it worked. At the end I took a step back, shook his hand, looked him in the eye and said: 'You're fit and you're strong.' And he knew it.

"By the end he was as good at some exercises as footballers who had been doing them for a couple of years. If you get his trust, he will do anything for you – he would walk through walls. I've got time for Stephen – as much time as he wants."

A few weeks later, Winsper was lazing at home in front of the television and flicked on *Sky Sports News*. It was the fourth morning of the first Test between West Indies and England at Sabina Park. "I didn't have the channel showing the game, so I sat and watched the news bulletins. He started taking wickets and it was fantastic. I kept shouting to my wife: 'He's taken another, he's taken another!' In the end his final figures came through and I was jumping about the living room."

Harmison was applauded off the Jamaica pitch by his team-mates and disappeared into the pavilion. Shortly afterwards, Winsper's phone beeped. It was a text message, all the way from the Caribbean. "That's for you", it said. Almost a year later Winsper still had the message on his phone.

Then Winsper began receiving texts from a string of players in the Newcastle squad who had heard the news. "Lots of them had begun to follow Stephen's career. The next day at work that's all people were talking about."

The squad signed a Newcastle shirt, with the figures 7-12

on the back, and sent it out to the Caribbean. On his return to the north-east, the Durham bowler was invited to a match at St James' and paraded on the pitch at half-time.

As for Winsper, he would later receive "some fantastic letters from the ECB, from people like Hugh Morris", thanking him for his contribution. Harmison himself, though, handed over the most precious treasure of them all.

"He had two match shirts from Sabina Park and he's given me one of them. He's labelled them 7-12 (1) and 7-12 (2). He's given me the second one, all signed by the England team and with his name on it.

"That means more to me than anything he or the ECB could have paid me for carrying out his conditioning training, without a doubt."

Looking back, many felt there were some serious lessons to be learnt from the Newcastle story. How was it that a cricketer could so rapidly be transformed simply by visiting a football club? Hussain, now a member of the cricketing media, says the case adds volume to the age-old lament that county cricket is based on a damaging diet of quantity rather than quality.

"It's a worrying thing that Steve Harmison sits in county cricket for almost 10 years and has a certain level of fitness, then two months with Newcastle football club and his level of fitness has gone up six-fold," he says.

"The problem is just too much cricket. All the coaches can do is get the lad on the park. He bowls, and then it's in the car and off to the next match. There's no actual assessment of how he's bowling, his wrist position, how his fitness is, what he has to work on. There's no time."

Harmison's case, indeed, has direct echoes with that of his close friend Flintoff a few years before. To an extent, both were their own worst enemies as young men, with a predilection for 'pop and pies' and a questionable commitment to personal fitness. Flintoff once ballooned to such a size that he weighed more than world heavyweight boxing champion Lennox Lewis. But the county grind did not help.

"When Freddie got into the England side he had been at Lancashire for ten years," says Hussain. "These young players get into the England set-up and England have to start afresh with them, getting them really fit, when in fact they should turn up at England almost the finished article. That includes everything, such as the slower ball, the wrist position, the run-up, the action.

"But in county cricket you just play cricket all the time. You're absolutely knackered. To tell Steve Harmison after a four-dayer, a Benson and Hedges game and a Sunday league game to go to the gym and do all this work... well, you can't."

The case of both players, now the national team's most prized match-winning assets, also raises questions over how England monitor their squad. When Flintoff was ruled out of the 2002-3 Ashes after failing to get fit following his hernia operation, The ECB chairman, Lord McLaurin, suggested the player himself was to blame, adding that a footballer would have returned within three or four months. Many, however, felt England's monitoring of the player bore as much responsibility. In 2005, Harmison and England would find themselves in a not dissimilar situation, barely a year after his career-defining achievements in the West Indies.

CHAPTER TWELVE

GBH

Nobody saw Steve Harmison coming, that morning. It had broken bright and blue, promising little more or indeed little less than any other sleepy Jamaican Sunday. But by early afternoon the day had been wrenched clean off its axis. March 14, 2004 became one of those historic "where were you?" sort of days. The place to be – as long as you weren't padded up and with your name on the West Indies team sheet – was the Sabina Park cricket ground in Kingston.

There had been no premonition of the whirlwind to come. God-fearing Jamaicans ambled quietly home from morning church, while their cricket-worshipping neighbours headed for the game in high spirits, anticipating a long, meandering day of entertainment. In England, David Graveney was at home, about to enjoy a Sunday lunch with his family. Steve Williams, Harmison's first coach, was setting off on holiday to visit his daughter. Williams's son Greg, Steve's friend and former team-mate, had a children's cricket coaching clinic to attend to.

The First Test between West Indies and England was perfectly balanced that fourth morning. There seemed to be plenty more cricket left in the match. Even the experts were to be caught unawares. One British cricket journalist, gambling on a fallow period of play before lunch, had even accepted the offer of an early-morning round of golf. His colleagues would fill him in, if a wicket happened to fall.

A few weeks before, England had arrived in the Caribbean convinced that they had a good chance of making history. They had not won an away series against West Indies for 36 years, long before most of the team had been born. They had, however, beaten their opponents in their previous home series. That 3-1 victory in 2000 had suggested an end of an era, the contest marking Ambrose's retirement. Walsh, the last of a great generation of West Indian pacemen, would continue for eight months longer before hanging up his well-worn boots.

Neither side, this time, could boast such eminent firepower. Lara's side contained two bustling young quicks in Tino Best and Fidel Edwards, but they were largely untried. Vaughan's bowlers also had things to prove. Harmison had recorded personal-best performances in his last two games but, back from his 'mystery' injury, had fences to mend and convincing to do. Simon Jones would play his first game since wrecking his knee in Australia, 16 months before. Hoggard, after struggling in Sri Lanka, could not be sure of a starting place ahead of Anderson.

The first three days of the First Test had been heavy on attrition and short on flamboyance as both sides dug in for the series. England were understandably cautious. The last time they had played at Sabina Park, in January 1998, the match had lasted 10.1 overs. Ambrose and Walsh, exploiting the vagaries of a newly-laid track, had reduced the touring side to 17 for three and hit the batsmen so often that the England physio had spent more time on than off the pitch, administering ice and pain-killing spray, before the umpires ruled the pitch unplayable and abandoned the game.

There was no such misbehaviour this time, though, as both sides passed 300 on their first visits. West Indies, winning the toss, had recovered to 311 after losing their four most experienced batsmen (Chris Gayle, Ramnaresh Sarwan, Lara and Shivnarine Chanderpaul) for a combined total of 35 runs. Devon Smith compensated with a century while Ryan Hinds, returning to the side, like his partner, after a lengthy absence, made 84 batting at six. All the English bowlers chipped in, Hoggard the mainstay with three for 68. Harmison, inducing a string of edges while never settling on either the Blue Mountains End or the Headley Stand End, took two wickets.

England, in reply, managed to eke out a slim first-innings advantage while suffering a high-speed grilling from the slingy Edwards and the scowling, ranting Best. Edwards, mixing bouncers with yorkers, had reduced the touring side to 33 for two before Hussain and Butcher, who had both been in the 1998 side along with Thorpe, kept their heads down and clung on for half-centuries, Butcher doing so with a thousand bells ringing inside his head after being struck on the side of the helmet by Best. Hoggard was almost as impressive at the end of the innings. Once he had been a rabbit with no shots, but now he was a barnacle with, admittedly, no shots. He hung around for 71 balls to help England sneak ahead.

The second and third days had been spattered by rain. The fourth dawned fine, West Indies 20 runs behind with all 10 second-innings wickets standing. Lara knew that England would have the disadvantage of batting last on a deteriorating surface. Bat out the penultimate day, he told his troops, and they would hold the upper hand.

England, though, were confident. They had enjoyed plenty of success against recent West Indian sides and suspected that they might lack the stomach for a fight if early inroads could be made. Twice in their last four Tests, England had exposed West Indian batting frailties. At Lord's in 2000, in the days of Gough and Caddick, they had bowled them out for 54. A month later at Headingley it was 61.

Harmison, meanwhile, had been doing his homework. Best and Edwards had hit speeds approaching 94mph in the first innings and the temptation must have been to answer in kind but Cooley sat him down and discussed lengths. It was a fast and lively surface still. The Hawkeye readings suggested, as so often in Harmison's career, that he needed to pitch the ball further up. The pair decided he did not need to bowl flat out but he needed to bowl full.

The ground was still filling up when England took to the field. Most of the crowd were looking back, not forwards. Sunday morning's papers were splashed with Best's face after he had taken three high-speed wickets on the third day, in so doing reviving dimmed memories of past Caribbean glories. The likes of Ambrose and Walsh – and 'Whispering Death' Michael Holding, now a television commentator – had been tall, long, loose-limbed athletes. Men of few words and limited facial animation, they had loped and glided lazily across the grass, lining up batsmen through sharks' eyes. Best, a bouncing rubber-ball of a man, could not have been more different. He was short and stocky and bursting with muscular energy, quick to taunt and ready with theatrical wicket-taking celebrations. On the third day, he had thrown himself on his back and, arms in the air, had awaited his team-mates' adulation after one success.

What Harmison made of such antics is anyone's guess. The Sabina Park crowd, however, loved it. Their cricket had lacked substance for several years but here at least was some in-your-face style. Nose down in those Sunday newspapers, the spectators may not have noticed England's strike bowler making his way to his mark for the start of the fourth day, a tall, long, loose-limbed man of few words.

West Indies resumed on eight for no wicket. Harmison had bowled eight balls on the previous evening before bad light had halted play. By the time he had cleaned up his unfinished

158

over, West Indies had moved on to 12, Smith, the first-innings centurion, edging the ball low and through the slips to the boundary.

Hoggard, bowling at a fresh fast-medium from the Blue Mountains End, then set out his stall with a near-perfect over. In the drama that was to follow, it was easy to forget the Yorkshireman's contribution. Not only was he to take two big wickets but he helped create a mood of foreboding from the very start. Bowling over the wicket at Chris Gayle, the right-armer aimed for an off-stump line while swinging it back in to the left-hander. Gayle, a tall man of huge and lavish power, favoured the back-foot cut and drive, but Hoggard, England's yeoman, kept drawing him forward. To keep Gayle guessing, Hoggard speared one ball straight across him as he began with a maiden.

The next over was a maiden as well, although Harmison, still getting into his rhythm, ended it with a shake of the head, knowing he had not made Smith play enough at the new ball. Hoggard continued the pattern with another vice-tight over.

By then, the crowd, without a single shot to cheer, had gone quiet. Gayle, facing Harmison, decided enough was enough and aimed an expansive back-foot slash. The ball, just back of a length, was wide enough but not quite short enough. The ball caught up with Gayle as he tried to get through with the stroke and fizzed off the edge to third slip where Thorpe got both hands to a head-height howitzer that almost knocked him off his feet. A quarter of an hour had gone and England had made the first breach. The Sabina band started up in defiance, but the crowd failed to join in.

The next half-an-hour was to decide the match. In all, five wickets fell for eight runs in 42 balls, three to Harmison and two to Hoggard. The Durham man, concentrating on pitching the ball just back of a length and on an off-stump line, got the first three, by which time he looked impossible to score off. Sarwan's second ball from Harmison had spat off a length and made the batsman snap back his head in alarm, to gasps from the tribunes. The West Indies number three soon found himself contemplating another over from the England strike bowler as Smith, perhaps wisely, opted to stay put at the other end. Encircled by three slips, two gullies, a point and a short leg, Sarwan hopped about for five deliveries before falling to the sixth as the ball, angled in on his leg stump, thudded into his pads. Sarwan returned to the pavilion with only the second pair of his Test career.

Harmison had bowled two consecutive wicket-maidens. The next over was almost as good. Smith stole a single off his glove before Chanderpaul became his next victim. Flinching to get out of the way of a ball aimed at his ribs, he was struck on the arm guard first ball. Crab-like, he tried to scuttle forward to the next but failed to bring his bat down straight and the ball squeezed through off the edge and into the stumps to make it 15 for three.

Lara had been watching proceedings with increasing dismay from the pavilion. He had opted to push himself down the order from four to five after dislocating a finger while fielding and had begun the day in his maroon West Indies track-suit, slouching back in a chair. The early clatter of wickets had sent him rushing inside to change, however, and Chanderpaul's fall brought him out to the middle.

It needed something special from the West Indies captain but he failed to provide it. He posed theatrically after blocking Harmison's final ball of the over but Lara did not survive long enough to get another look at him. Hoggard squared him up next over and induced an edge into Flintoff's bucket-shaped hands. It was the first time that Sarwan, Lara and Chanderpaul had all been dismissed for ducks in the same Test innings.

One over later Hoggard struck again as Smith drove back at the bowler. The shot was miscued but the ball was travelling. "It's a case of catch it or wear it," Botham said in his television commentary. Hoggard caught it, two-handed, just next to his Adam's apple, before slinging the ball into the air in celebration. West Indies were 21 for five, 50 minutes after the start of play, with Hinds and Jacobs at the crease, neither having faced a ball.

At that stage, England's two opening bowlers had similar figures, Harmison with 7-4-10-3 to Hoggard's 7.3-2-11-2. Hoggard, though, would only bowl one more completed over while no one could prise the ball out of Harmison's grasp. Every time he looked as if he was tiring, his hair glistening with sweat in the morning heat, he somehow conjured up another wicket to earn another over. In all, that morning, he bowled 11.1 overs on the reel. "I don't know what they did for him (at Newcastle)," Vaughan said later, "but he's arrived in the Caribbean full of fitness and full of enthusiasm."

The same could not be said of the West Indian batsmen. Hinds, like Smith, showed he had the technique to survive but not to score. Jacobs would risk all in scoring but lacked the technical expertise to stay for long. The wicket-keeper, quick on to the front foot, clouted two straight boundaries off Hoggard and picked up Jones and drove him straight for a one-bounce four as well. Harmison, though, was not short enough to pull or full enough to drive. Jacobs, caught in no-man's land, was struck on the shoulder before a wild lash rocketed to gully where Collingwood, on as the substitute fielder, dived right and got both hands to the chance only for the ball to bounce clear as he fell.

Vaughan must have been on the brink of offering Harmison a well-earned break but his next over made that impossible. The stocky Jacobs, softened up by a bouncer, gloved the next ball straight up into the air and Hussain ran from short leg to pouch the catch. Best nearly lost his head as the next ball exploded off a length, then lost his wicket as he backed off and deflected behind to give wicket-keeper Chris Read as easy a catch as he will ever take. That made it 41 for seven and the end was suddenly in sight. Thorpe hardly delayed matters next ball by losing sight of a routine slip chance off Adam Sanford, which would have put Harmison on a hat-trick. Within 21 more balls, the innings was over.

Jones had Hinds caught behind off a front-foot drive and Harmison, pitching the ball up at the tail-enders, induced two catches to first slip to take his 49th and 50th Test wickets and wrap up the innings.

West Indies had been dismissed for 47 in 25.3 overs. It was their lowest score in history, their previous low a 51 against the Australians at Port of Spain five years before. Harmison's career-defining figures, 12.3-8-12-7, were the best by any bowler at Sabina Park, surpassing Trevor Bailey's seven for 34 half a century earlier, as well as a career best. It recalled the day, almost 10 years previously, when West Indies had bowled England out for 46 in 19.1 overs in Trinidad, with Ambrose taking six for 24. Others remembered another historic Ambrose burst, when he had taken seven wickets for a single run against the Australians in Perth in 1993, on the way to figures of 18-9-25-7.

Amidst a flotilla of statistics, though, it was the images and sounds of the day that stayed in the mind. Once, Caribbean crowds were renowned for never-ending noise and gaiety, their Calypso rhythm beaten out with empty beer cans. But at Sabina Park, on March 14, 2004, they sat in near silence, as if at a wake, leaving the Barmy Army to fill the vacuum with their own soundtrack.

For English fans, the unforgettable image was provided by a slip cordon stretching out further than their minds could comprehend. By the end, Read had a ribbon of seven men spread out to his right as Harmison came thundering in. There was also a fly slip, placed some 30 yards behind that line, waiting for a top edge that might clear the trap. The other fielder, defending the rest of the field, was Hussain at short leg.

Perhaps the most telling picture, however, came right at the end. Edwards had snicked to slip and the innings was over. The fielders had congregated around Harmison in a tight gaggle of disbelief, high-fiving and slapping each other on the back to make sure they were awake. The team then turned for the changing rooms. Harmison, reverting to type, slunk quietly back in to the safety of the group, attempting to look as anonymous as a 6ft 4ins man, fresh from making history, can appear in a sparse crowd of shorter men. He did not succeed in staying there long, a sharp shove in the back from Flintoff propelling him out in front of his team-mates.

The fast bowler examined his boots and fidgeted with his hat on the way back to the pavilion but knew there was nowhere to hide. He looked about, brushed his nose a couple of times at a non-existent irritant, then finally acknowledged the applause, with a couple of almost apologetic half-waves of the hand, before hurrying into the sanctuary of the pavilion.

England took just 15 balls to score the 20 needed for victory, leaving the captains to try to make sense of what had happened. Vaughan hailed it as "one of the greatest ever spells by an England bowler", adding: "The wicket was bouncing, there was a little bit of movement; he just made it very, very uncomfortable for batting. I always ask myself: 'Would I have liked to be batting out there?' And the answer would have been no.

"It was surreal. I fully expected two more hard days of Test cricket. I thought we might be able to bowl them out for around 200 but expected it to be difficult."

Lara, understandably, did not want to dwell on the wreckage. "The guys will have to erase this from their memory," he said.

Harmison – GBH, or Grievous Bodily Harmison, as one tabloid had once ironically nicknamed him for the damage he was prone to inflict on his team-mates in the nets rather than on opponents – seemed as bemused. "It's unbelievable, really. I feel a bit numb at the minute.

"I am speechless. I cannot say much about what happened. I have worked hard since the tour of Bangladesh with some good people in some good places and they have helped me a lot, so I want to thank them."

By the end of his press conference, however, he was less amused after learning that Newcastle United had lost 1-0 at Tottenham. Freelance journalist Simon Cambers, covering the tour for Reuters, remembers: "That happened quite a few times during the tour – we were interviewing him about the cricket and he wanted to know about the football. He had often had a good day on the field but seemed more affected by what had happened to Newcastle."

Back home, there was the same sense of incredulity. The Sabina Park match had not been on terrestrial television, so few had seen the drama unfold. Greg Williams recalls: "I was taking a coaching session for some kids and one of the parents came over and said Steve had taken seven for 12. I didn't believe it. I thought it was a wind-up."

Greg's father Steve was in a London hotel, waiting for a flight to Menorca to visit his daughter who had just had a baby. The hotel did not have Sky Sports and neither did the pub down the road, so he stayed glued to the sports news channel. "I was absolutely gutted. Every 20 minutes they gave you updates. I rang his dad up when it was all over but I couldn't get through, there was such a party going on up there."

Harmison's former teacher, Kieran McGrane, was pottering around school. "One of our caretakers, a guy called John Haig, who's very big in cricket around the Ashington area, came to find me to pass it on. We always get the cricket updates from John. I tend to bump into him when I'm walking around school and I invariably ask: 'How's the cricket going, and how's Stephen doing?' It was pretty much all over when he found me. John came up and said: 'You won't believe this.'"

Graveney, meanwhile, recalls: "I was having Sunday lunch with my family. I was watching it on the TV. The rest of my family were leaping about, but perhaps I'm a bit more battle-hardened. I was pleased for the team more than anything else. We've played Test matches that have ended in success but they have always been a bit in the balance as the game has gone on; it's not been like Australia scoring 500 and then bashing through and wrapping things up quickly. The games have made for compulsive viewing but have been hard to watch, depending what position you are in. It was over before it began, really."

Harmison's figures at Sabina Park, extraordinary as they were, fell between several stools. They failed to feature in the best statistics in Test history – two men, Jim Laker of England and Anil Kumble of India, have taken 10 wickets in a single innings while a plethora of players have taken nine and eight – and they also failed to make the lists for top innings averages or economy rates. As a combination of wicket taking, average per wicket and economy per over, however, his performance must rank as one of the best. No one, certainly, has ever taken seven wickets in a Test match more cheaply. Three men, Monty Noble of Australia and John Briggs and Wilfred Rhodes of England, each took 7-17 between 1888 and 1902, but no one had bettered those performances for more than a century until Harmison came along.

All ten of the West Indies' wickets fell within one hour and 28 minutes. First to last, it took 108 deliveries or 18 overs, during which 34 runs were scored. There were five ducks. Only three batsmen got beyond three and only two reached double figures.

Harmison contributed two wicket maidens and one double wicket maiden. In all, he conceded five scoring shots off 75 deliveries. At least three of those were involuntary. Two were edged for four low through the slips (both by Smith), while a single came off the glove (also Smith's). The three 'voluntary' runs came from a Smith tip-and-run to cover and a Ryan Hinds front-foot mistimed drive through mid-on for a couple, when all the fielders bar Hussain and Simon Jones were behind the bat.

He did not bowl a wide or a no-ball, but conceded two leg byes off a single ball. Harmison's first three wickets came within 14 balls and cost one run (off Smith's glove). His last four wickets were taken in 13 balls for no run.

He bowled at ten of the 11 West Indian batsmen, with Corey Collymore the odd one out. Eight of those ten failed to score off him. None of his seven victims scored off him.

Smith showed the most defiance, facing 27 Harmison deliveries without being dismissed and making ten runs. Hinds faced 12 balls without being dismissed for two runs. Brian Lara also survived but only faced one ball, which he blocked. Of the victims, Gayle fell to his fourth ball from the Durham bowler while Sarwan lasted eight, Chanderpaul two (he was hit on the armguard off the first delivery), Jacobs nine (he was hit on the helmet off the second and dropped off the third), Best two, Sanford six (he was dropped off the first) and Edwards four.

Harmison struck four batsmen about the body during his spell (Gayle, Chanderpaul, Smith and Jacobs). To cap it all, he also saw two catches dropped. The first would have been brilliant, the second was a sitter. Nine of Harmison's deliveries, too short or too wide, were wasted. The rest all counted. There were four bouncers and 23 short deliveries to keep the batsmen pinned back and under siege, 33 deliveries just back of a length and 15 balls full-pitched. Three wickets fell to balls just back of a length, three to full-length deliveries and one to a short ball. Crucially, he bowled near-perfect lines throughout, so that the batsmen were always in the line of fire.

Several men were well placed to witness Harmison's performance at Sabina Park but no one, not even the bowler himself, had a better situation than Daryl Harper.

"That has to be the most impressive piece of bowling I have seen at close quarters," the Australian umpire said. "I have seen others take five or six, but seven for 12 in just under 13 overs, with no one, absolutely no one, taking to him, well… That was the thing – they just couldn't get a bat on him.

"Everything seemed to fall into place. He's a big gangly sort of guy. Sometimes he looks more awkward than at other times, but on that particular day he seemed to find a magical line and length. Several of them were balls that the batsmen could do nothing about.

"It was quite unreal. Once the rot started, there was no way it was going to stop. It just seemed like an unstoppable force charging through them, just a matter of time."

Harper doesn't think the West Indians had seen much of Harmison before as a bowler. Neither had he. "I didn't know a lot about him at all. There had been a few one-dayers, and I umpired the South Africa series in England, but he didn't do anything remarkable. I was also on the Sri Lanka tour but he missed it. My impression was that he had potential but that I hadn't seen him deliver it."

Beforehand, Harper may have caught a glimpse of Harmison in the nets or around the hotel but they would have exchanged little more than a passing word. "Umpires usually go into the nets a couple of days before a Test match, just to say hello to the bowlers and reacquaint themselves with them or with anyone new. We like to see where they bowl from at the crease and just to try and get a feel for the track and the bounce, assuming it will be similar out in the middle.

"Stephen is one of those guys who will always have a friendly word, whether it be at breakfast in the hotel or whether he's just finished his spell. He's that sort of easy-going character and he's obviously a country boy. That stands out. He's very straightforward, very honest. He just lopes along. He doesn't come over as a hardened city kid.

"I don't know if that's the teacher in me coming out, perhaps, making that assessment. I was a teacher for 23 years, teaching in the city and the country. I just appreciated his outlook and the way he responded to me."

Harper remembers that the match was evenly poised on the fourth morning. Harmison had started the match bowling from Billy Bowden's end "without doing anything very exciting." The Sabina Park track had produced 300-odd runs for each side "so it wasn't a shocker. There were no bowlers' marks to cause discomfort.

"It was just that he had one of those days when he could do no wrong. It was pretty much the same delivery that caused all the trouble, just a fraction short of a length with more bounce than they expected. He has that much more height than any of the others. He seems to bring the ball down from about six inches higher. Freddie gets a bit of bounce but Matthew Hoggard and Simon Jones skid it through."

Harper was struck by several things as Harmison began to make inroads. There was the quietness of the crowd – "I had expected them to be a lot more rowdy" – and a sense of inevitability that rapidly built up. There was also an absence of any sort of malice or open hostility in the bowler's demeanour.

"It was just a matter of all the pieces fitting into place, like the parts of a jigsaw, that perfect length that he found, with a bit of movement off the track. The batsmen were all at sea. They were just looking to survive, it was no more than self-preservation, really. Not that he was bouncing the ball towards their heads or anything like that. Some were just outside off stump and they could have been allowed to pass, they weren't all going to hit the stumps. But he lured them in, he had them trapped in that negative mindset."

The delivery that dismissed Jacobs stood out. "Jacobs got one off the glove and he could not have fended it off in any other way. The ball just reared off a length," says Harper.

"Some bowlers, such as Glenn McGrath, have a mean streak, but I can't recall Steve at any time having a word to a batsman. It's not part of his armoury. He does it with the ball rather than with his mouth. There was no nastiness coming out because, basically, he hasn't got any in him. He seems a bit of a gentle giant to me but, after all, cricket is a gentleman's game. Just because the Australians sledge, it doesn't mean that's the way to go."

England, indeed, seemed too focussed and intent on their work to bother with chatter that day. "It was their confidence that struck me. Thorpe missed a sitter in the slips but no one was fazed by it. It was: 'Oh well, let's get the next one.' There was no concern. There was no doubt he was going to run right through them, especially when he knocked over the top order. The lower order just started fending him off. There was no way they wanted to get in line behind the ball."

It proved an easy session to umpire for Harper, despite the never-ending clatter of wickets. "You just knew something was going to happen more often than not. In some games, where guys put on 100 or 150, you anticipate something is going to happen but the danger is that your concentration can flag a little. But because it was such a short spell, I'm sure that helped channel the concentration.

"He earned all those wickets. He could have had eight with that catch going down to Thorpe, but he didn't worry about that, he just came back in.

"That's what I have enjoyed about having him bowl at my end. Whether he gets knocked about or not, it is always the same positive attitude. He has a warm approach, to me as an umpire but to the other guys as well. Nothing seems to faze him."

The other thing Harper remembers was the inordinate amount of time he spent that morning exchanging pleasantries with his fellow umpire, the New Zealander Bowden.

"As an umpire, you stand out there doing a professional job but you also have to be impressed with those sort of performances. I think we were just stunned. There was the feeling the Test might finish a bit early, but to wrap it up so quickly... We hadn't planned to pack up so fast and leave for Trinidad.

"You meet at the fall of every wicket. We wandered across and it was basically: 'See you at the next one.' We knew it wouldn't be far away. Some matches, you don't see much of each other. But at Sabina there was just this overpowering feeling that we would be back for a chat in a short while. Billy likes a bit of a chat, as I do. We had plenty of them."

Chris Read was the man at the other end of the pitch. He had got up that morning expecting another tough session after the opening two days of evenly matched sparring.

"No one saw it coming, that's for sure," said the wicket-keeper. "We had scrapped hard to lead by 20 or 30 after the first innings, with the middle order really having to dig in. It was a good cricket wicket, probably with the most bounce that I had seen since I had begun playing at Test level. It had good pace and terrific carry. I was standing a long way back.

"We all came out that day thinking we would need to work hard to get a few early breakthroughs. We felt that if we could get them six down, we could roll them over. So the first priority was to get rid of the top order, then we would be in business."

After the first three overs, Read felt the wicket had actually improved for batting and he gritted his teeth at the prospect of a long day stretching out in front of him. "Then all of a sudden the first wicket went and the procession started," he says. "It was an absolutely unbelievable spell of bowling."

Read had played with Harmison at Under-19 level and played against him in county matches. "He was always a very uncomfortable bowler to face but the overriding criticism was that he didn't get enough balls in the right place. At Sabina, though, there was a marked difference. He was getting 11 out of 12 there. There was nowhere for the batsmen to go. He was also getting some away swing."

Read says he is not the type to reflect too much on the past "but I still can't believe how the wickets just kept on falling. You get big collapses in county cricket but you always seem to get a partnership somewhere along the line, even if it's only for 40-odd runs between a couple of tail-enders. This time, though, it never happened. You thought there would come a time when Harmy would want a rest and they would cobble together around 150 or so. You just don't see things like that."

Like Harper, he found his senses sharpened, rather than overwhelmed, by the speed of events. "It certainly wasn't hard to concentrate, quite the opposite in fact. I felt a catch could be coming every ball. It was the perfect session. Later, I saw a photograph of eight men lined up in our slip cordon. That image has stayed with me."

After it was all over, he says, there was a short period of reflection. "People took a while to figure out what had happened. It all felt a bit surreal. Everybody thought the game would go to five days."

Then the celebrations began. "It was fairly raucous. I can't remember whether we threw Harmy in the ice bath – perhaps we didn't, knowing his aversion to them. We didn't stay too long in the dressing room – they are a bit gloomy at Sabina. We just had a few beers and then continued around the swimming pool. We had had a tough few weeks preparing in Jamaica and there we were, with a day-and-a-half off. We were elated. Fletch (Duncan Fletcher) is good like that. When we win, we celebrate properly. We don't undervalue a victory."

Many wicket-keepers have referred to the difficulties of keeping to Harmison but he was a dream that day, says Read. "It definitely felt like a bit of history. The whole tour felt like that for me. It was my first long tour. We really knew we had a good chance of winning in the West Indies.

"I'll never forget the first three games. If I never play for England again, those three Tests will stay with me forever as the best cricket that I have been involved in.

"Harmy? Well, everyone was jumping about afterwards, trying to come to terms with what he had achieved, and he just kept going on about a mobile phone text he had got from Alan Shearer, as if that was the most exciting thing about the day."

For match umpire Mike Procter, the day brought back some painful memories. The former all-rounder had been South Africa's coach on August 20, 1994 at The Oval, when Devon Malcolm, a true batting rabbit but spitting with fury after being clanged on the helmet by a Fanie de Villiers bouncer, had produced a furious performance worthy of comparison. "You guys are history," he was supposed to have said after the blow to his head, before taking a match-winning nine for 57.

"That was a magic bit of bowling as well, it was superb. But Malcolm only managed to do it once," says Procter. "He was a good quick bowler and he got wickets from time to time but he never produced another sustained performance like that. Harmison was excellent throughout the series in the West Indies.

"What struck me about him was his rhythm. He is very much a rhythm bowler. His action is a little bit awkward, he has to get his run-up and timing just right. But on that day he got it spot on. He was really quick and looked the best bowler in the world.

"I had seen him a couple of times before, when he seemed to be a bit of an in-or-out bowler. What I think has happened is that he has got it more consistently right than before. I remember his constant pace and aggression, and his line and length. He really looked like everything was under control. He seemed to get everything right. He pushed deliveries up, he whacked the ball in short. It really was top quality.

"You don't get many fast bowlers who can take seven for 12!"

Apart from the West Indies batsmen, Hussain is the other man capable of offering a first-hand, close-up account of Harmison's Jamaican demolition. Crouching low at short leg, he could almost feel the air currents as each ball whistled past him at head height. It also gave him a perfect view.

After the game, Hussain shared a drink with Brian Lara.

"I get on very well with Brian. We have known each other a long time. To hear someone like Lara say that the English bowlers were making him jump around was great. 'You have to get past Hoggard, and he tests your technique,' he was saying. 'Then there's Harmison to survive, and Jones, and then Flintoff comes on and he's making me dance about as well.' "

Hussain had been hoping for some early England successes, if only because he did not relish the thought of another tussle with Best and Edwards on a deteriorating surface. "The pitch started alright. Smith got his hundred and played really well, but, from the moment it dried, it started to get quicker and there was some uneven bounce to contend with. Butch and I had to play out of our skins just to get 50 or 60-odd each in the first innings. That spell from Best and Edwards, when we were 33 for two, was almost as torrid as any I have faced in my career, including spells from Allan Donald, Shoaib Akhtar and Brett Lee.

"But we fancied our chances. In recent years West Indies had been the sort of side who you always knew could be bowled out cheaply once in a game, if only you get through one or two of them."

What was to follow felt "almost like a role reversal", says Hussain.

"Generally in the West Indies we used to go there with pea shooters. Then you would go out to bat and have four fast bowlers coming at you. There would be the roar of the crowd and the band playing. They love their 'chin music' – they would go wild even after a mediocre bouncer. But this time, apart from Best and Edwards, they were hitting us with medium-pacers while we were hitting them with Harmison, backed up by Jones and Flintoff.

"At one stage I was the only bloke in front of square. Obviously Harmy wasn't going to fetch the ball, so anything hit in around a 190-degree arc was mine. Here's this 36-year-old, with all the protective gear on, having to run in 40-degree heat to get the ball back. So I was quite pleased they weren't hitting anything.

"I was stuck at short leg seeing the fear in their eyes and for me it was great, after years of England being on the other end. I was brought up on watching Gatting and Gooch being pummelled. Even on my first tour of the West Indies I was fending it off against Patrick Patterson. Then you had to watch Greenidge and Haynes hitting it to all parts. And here I was at Sabina, with Lara and Sarwan jumping around, thinking: 'I've waited a long time for this.' So Harmy immediately became my number one person in the world."

Hussain, too, can remember the quiet, almost disbelieving start to England's celebrations.

"For me, the celebrations are always muted. I like to look around the dressing room. I like to see how people's lives are changing right before you. I had a look around and saw Harmy sitting calmly in his corner.

"He had a beer in his hand and he was getting texts from all over. He got a text from Shearer or someone, and his eyes lit up. He went around showing it to everyone. That meant more to him probably than anything his team-mates could say to him.

"That's what I like about the lad. He would never change. He can become the greatest bowler there has ever been and he won't change. I see him in the morning now and it's 'Morning Nasser, how are you doing?' Same old Steve Harmison."

Lara's plea that his players should erase Sabina Park from the collective memory bank seemed to work. On the opening morning of the Second Test in Trinidad, Harmison was belted out of the attack, West Indies raced along at four an over to 99 without loss, and the lunch menu looked inviting. All the home side needed to do was safely negotiate the final 10 minutes before the break.

With the first two matches running back-to-back, the West Indies had had little time to recover. The first thing they did after their Jamaican debacle was to issue an unprecedented public apology. A press release talked of the side's "shocking performance on the fourth day". Lara's hand had largely been forced when four of his players, including vice-captain Sarwan, had been spotted partying at Sabina Park shortly after the team's humiliation. But things looked a lot rosier after 24 overs at Queen's Park Oval in Port of Spain. It had not taken long for Gayle and Smith to deconstruct the Harmison myth as quickly as it had been established. Five overs into his first spell and the pair had already taken three fours and 14 runs off him, more than he had conceded in the entire second innings of the First Test. Gayle shrugged off a blow to the shoulder and rubbed things in with drives off both feet, and a pull, as he hit three boundaries off four balls, sending Harmison back to the fine leg boundary for a rethink.

After 12 overs, the West Indies had got to 48 without loss, in the process exorcising their Jamaican ghosts. Harmison was replaced by Giles, and Gayle celebrated the return of the good times by hammering him out of the attack as well, lofting him for a towering six as his half-century came up off 58 deliveries.

The next few minutes, however, were to go a long way to deciding the series. A bank of cloud had begun to build up. Harmison switched ends and was given time for a couple of overs before lunch. By the break, Gayle, Smith and Lara, for another four-ball duck, were all out and it was 110 for three.

Gayle had edged behind, Smith fell lbw to a leg-cutter as he remained rooted to the crease, and Lara, cheered to the crease moments before by the Trini Posse, received a brute that took the shoulder of his bat and sailed to gully. Lara trudged back, dismissed for a second duck in consecutive innings for the first time in a 104-Test career. Harmison, suddenly rediscovering his magical length, had taken three wickets for one run in eight balls.

Rain delayed the restart but could not disrupt Harmison. Indeed, all it seemed to do was freshen up a benign pitch.

"The thing I remember about Trinidad was that there was an instant transformation after the rain shower, recalls Read. "They got the covers on quickly but it really livened things up. When we went back on I was standing three yards further back. Suddenly it was flying."

Harmison, his dander up, shrugged off the occasional hiccup – Dwayne Smith had the temerity to pull him for six before attempting a repeat off his next ball and holing out at mid-wicket – and sliced clean through the top order, removing five of the first six batsmen. Sarwan completed his haul, roughed up with two bouncers and then snicking to the slips. Wicket to wicket, Harmison had taken five for 13 off 6.3 overs. The next day he returned to complete figures of six for 61 off 20.1 overs and West Indies had crumbled to 208 all out.

For the bowler himself, it had been an even better performance than in the first Test. "I honestly think I bowled better than I did on Sunday," he said. "I think I put the ball in better areas."

He had also achieved this on the first day of a Test, on a pristine wicket. Psychologically, too, Trinidad was probably even more important. His first performance had left him speechless and numb, he said. The repeat just proved that it had not been a one-off. It also demonstrated that he could dismiss top-class batsmen who were now suddenly looking out for him, and not the other way around.

"I think when you get two or three quick wickets, and it's the same people as on Sunday, there is certainly more in their minds than in mine," he said. "To get someone like Brian Lara – one of the best batsmen in the world – gives you an extra kick."

Lara got yet another kicking in the second innings, when he fell to Harmison again, this time for eight. By then England's senior pros, Hussain, Butcher and Thorpe, had knuckled down again to deliver the touring side a 108-run lead. Simon Jones inherited the role of arch-destroyer in the second innings, taking his first five-wicket haul in Tests, and England were celebrating the retention of the *Wisden* Trophy early on the fifth day after chasing down 99 for victory.

Harmison, not surprisingly, was unable to keep pulling rabbits out of the hat in the Third and Fourth Tests. England, though, won again in Barbados, thanks to a Test-best of five for 58 from Flintoff and a back-to-the-wall unbeaten century from Thorpe. Harmison still contributed six wickets in the game and, batting at number 11, hung around for 39 runs with Thorpe. But the headline-grabbing fireworks came from Hoggard, who all but settled the game with a high-class hat-trick in the West Indies second innings. The home side, on 45 for two and still hoping to set England a challenging target, lost Sarwan, Chanderpaul and Hinds without adding a run and the series was gone.

Lara was left with a magnificent consolation in the final game as he became the first man to score 400 in an innings in Test history, ten years after he had claimed the world mark for the first time on the same ground. His extraordinary innings at St John's was another sign of the man's genius but, significantly, it was not enough to win the game, even if it did prevent the whitewash. England, 'chasing' 751 for five declared, wobbled in the first innings as they were dismissed for 285, but Vaughan steadied nerves with 140 in the second innings while the rest of the top four scored half-centuries to play out the draw on a featherbed pitch. Harmison, despite the Antigua anti-climax, ended with the man-of-the-series award for his 23 wickets at 14.86 runs apiece. Hoggard was his nearest challenger on either side, with 13 at a fraction over 25 each.

The one-day series was shared after rain had blighted the start. By now Harmison's star had waned significantly. One-dayers were still not his forte and he was already thinking of home after an historic tour.

"Just before the families came out to the West Indies, I struggled for a week and then later, through the one-dayers. It was horrendous," he later told Simon Wilde of *The Sunday Times.* "I struggled to be there. Maybe it was that the family had gone home and everything had gone with the Tests, but I'd had enough.

"It will always be there, even when I'm 30. I miss home. I can't put my finger on it. Some people are afraid of the dark, some scared of heights. I talk to Steve Bull (the team's psychologist) about it all the time... I'm fine in groups. It's when you are by yourself that you've time to think about it. I'm getting quite good at hiding it."

England were still hoping to turn him into a middle-overs wicket-taker but they experimented by giving him the ball from the start in St Lucia. It did not go well. He bowled four wides in his second over, snapped up Lara's wicket but was then hammered for two sixes and a four off his final over in conceding 74 off 10.

Taken in the context of the whole tour, however, the performance was a mere blip. Harmison left the Caribbean with a worldwide reputation. Homesickness, significantly, had not been mentioned once in the press. There had been too much else to concentrate on.

The one disappointment was that Harmison's bowling in the first two Tests had not reached a wider public back in England, due to the limited television coverage. Later some articles were to suggest, in an example of English self-deprecation, that perhaps his success has as much to do with lively pitches and dismal West Indian batting. There was some truth in those observations. But Gayle (Test average of 36 before the series), Sarwan (test average 39.41) and Chanderpaul (43.71) have never been widely seen as mugs before. And nobody argued after Lara's world-record romp in Antigua that, despite appearances and the latest world rankings, he wasn't really much of a batsman.

England had last won in the West Indies in 1967/8, when John Snow had taken 27 wickets at 18.66, including his best figures of seven for 49 at Sabina Park, against the likes of Gary Sobers, Clive Lloyd and that famous Ashington cricketer, Rohan Kanhai. It was only natural, therefore, that Harmison should return to a national hero's welcome and, considering the furore, perfectly natural too that the young man should lose all sense of perspective, move to a fashionable area, buy a sports car to advertise his new celebrity status and go rapidly off the rails.

Not that he did. Harmison returned home quietly and closed his front door firmly behind him. A few public appearances would follow but, for the most part, he spent time catching up with family and friends. There were a few rounds to get in at the RAOB men's social club. There were football and cricket mates to meet. Some of his final training sessions before the West Indies had been with Ashington Football Club, where his father was assistant manager. "It made us laugh, to think he was acclimatising for the Caribbean by slithering around with our players in three inches of mud," says club treasurer Tom Seely. "He still comes to watch our games when he's about."

Harmison was soon back at the cricket club as well, although his former team-mates had mixed feeling when he ambled up for net sessions. "He trundles in off a few paces but he never has a long bowl. Most of the team try to pad up before he arrives. More often, he just has a bat," says Greg Williams. "He's a really good crack."

Kieran McGrane, his former teacher, says the sudden recognition has changed nothing.

"I think he's quite measured. And one of the nice things

about him is that he is very happy in who he is, and I think that comes across clearly, that, as he has gone up the ladder, he doesn't seem to have changed to fit in with anybody or any group in particular.

"For me the good example of that is that he has bought a house in Ashington and he stays here. He has not moved out into a trendy part of, say, Newcastle. He knows where his roots are. You think of sports people nowadays and the first thing they do is to buy a flashy big house and a big car and throw their money around and get seen in silly places. Stephen is not like that. When he is home you are more likely to see him down the social club, having a pint and chatting with people normally. And that's what he wants, a normal life. I think that says a lot for him, that he's not trying to chase some sort of image of what a sports personality should be."

Even Cook finds himself surprised by the way Harmison manages to live out two very different lives. "When I think of Stephen I think of a huge paradox. The Harmisons are such a close family and there he is, spending so much time with them, caring for them, and on the other hand he's a world-class bowler. I remember his brother Ben was playing for the Durham Academy and Stephen just jogs up, the best bowler in the world, just lies on the grass, chews the cud and looks on. He's absolutely chilled out."

Interview anyone close to Harmison, and one phrase crops up continuously. "That's Harmy," they all say. He hasn't changed, they say, and he won't. That's how he is and you accept him as such.

Ashington Cricket Club hope their former bowler will return and play for them again, one day. For now, they must make do with him as a supporter (although he did come on as a emergency substitute fielder in a cup game following an injury to one of the team), watching their games from the pavilion steps as his two daughters play around him For now, they must try and fill his boots. In that regard, says team captain Greg Williams, they have had a little help.

"Our dressing room is like the England dressing room," he says. "Steve hands out caps to the young children and he brings us loads of gear back from his tours. I don't think there is a bowler in the team without a pair of his boots.

"They are size 13 or 14, of course, so some of them have to wear around five pairs of socks to get them to fit."

CHAPTER THIRTEEN

HARMISON HIP

New Zealand arrived for the 2004 series in England supremely confident. Many regarded it as one of the most competitive squads they had assembled for years. To boot, Stephen Fleming was being touted as the world's canniest captain. He, like coach John Bracewell, knew all about England, having enjoyed two stints playing county cricket. Bracewell had been the brains behind Gloucestershire's multiple one-day successes only a few seasons before.

Fleming also had winning form. He had led the squad to England in 1999 when New Zealand came from behind to take the Test series 2-1, in so doing dumping England at the bottom of the world rankings. The *Daily Telegraph*'s Michael Henderson had written the next day: "It is not true to say that England have the worst cricket team in the world. Even in their current state of disrepair, they would beat the Faroe Islands and give the Costa Ricans a run for their dollars, though there are worrying reports of strapping all-rounders emerging from Patagonia.") England's players, huddled in defeat and in a state of shock on The Oval pavilion balcony that day, were booed and heckled by their own fans with a serenade Hussain would long remember: "We've got the worst team in the world!"

Vaughan's side had just returned from the Caribbean and they found themselves with barely a fortnight to acclimatise for a home campaign. With a summer bursting at the seams with seven Tests and a raft of one-dayers as well as the Champions Trophy, the series was scheduled to start earlier than usual. Vaughan was well aware that if there were one side he would not choose to meet on a damp, early-season green-top, it would be the New Zealanders. The conditions would feel like home to them.

They were also showing good form. While England had won in the West Indies, New Zealand had given the South Africans a scare by holding them 1-1 in a home Test series and then routing them 5-1 in the one-dayers. Strike bowler Shane Bond seemed to be close to regaining full fitness following serious back problems while Chris Cairns, another man accustomed to English conditions, was determined to end his career on a high before retiring from Tests. In a perfect piece of stage management, the Third and last Test was to be played at Trent Bridge, the all-rounder's second home during a distinguished career with Nottinghamshire.

The New Zealanders also felt well briefed about their opponents. There was one unknown factor – Steve Harmison. A few of the tourists had played against SH Mark I, the pre-2003 version, in county cricket. Nobody, though, had come across SH Mark II.

Mark Richardson, New Zealand's opening batsman, recalls: "We had spoken about England's bowling and we had seen a bit of Harmison in Australia. Fleming and Cairns said he had some pace but that he was erratic and tended to lose it. There was talk that he had bowled well in the West Indies but that their batsmen had struggled to leave the ball. We weren't overly frightened at the prospect of Harmison – actually, we thought we would pick him off for some runs."

The series would prove to be a classic. Fleming and his side, hampered by a wardful of injuries, competed well in each game only to be blown away in the latter stages as England set off on an extraordinary record-breaking run of success.

Vaughan's side had already won three of their last four Tests and drawn the other, but better still was to come.

Vaughan's summer, however, began badly. Batting in the nets at Lord's in the run-up to the opening Test, he tumbled on his right knee. A hospital scan showed no significant injury but he was ruled out of the match. England thus went into battle with an uncapped opening batsman in Andrew Strauss and a stand-in leader in Marcus Trescothick. Fleming saw an opportunity to score early psychological points. Knowing Trescothick had had a poor time in the Caribbean, he remarked: "We've noticed that certain individuals are under a lot of pressure from the media. If Trescothick is one of those, it will be interesting to see how he takes to the extra responsibility."

Fleming, though, had targeted the wrong man. It was Strauss – and indeed Harmison – he should have been worrying about.

The first day at Lord's would be a microcosm of the series as the initiative swung one way and then the other. At 161 for one, New Zealand looked in control. Then three wickets fell for 13 runs either side of tea and the game was back in the balance. The tourists seemed to be regaining the initiative, with opener Richardson nearing three figures, when Harmison, gradually adjusting his length from the Caribbean, trapped him lbw shortly before the close.

"He hadn't bowled that well at the start," says Richardson. "But after the new ball lost its shine it began to swing about. That's when it suddenly got serious. He started smashing the ball into my hip and the rest of the bowlers paled by comparison."

The Durham player returned next day with three more wickets and a catch but barely earned a look-in as two batsmen caught the eye. First Cairns hammered an extraordinary 82 off 47 balls, including 10 fours and four sixes, in so doing surpassing Viv Richards's career record total of sixes hit in Tests. Then Strauss, playing on his home ground, re-wrote the story again, casting himself in the lead role.

First he became only the fourth player to score a Test century on debut at Lord's as he and Trescothick put on 190 for the first wicket. Then, on the brink of a second hundred as England neared victory on the final day, he was run out for 83 by Hussain. Hussain recomposed himself to score a match-sealing century of his own but, aware that Strauss might be dropped to make way for the returning Vaughan, he opted to hasten his own retirement, thus giving the selectors the easy option of retaining the younger man.

Hussain's departure and Strauss's extraordinary first waltz dominated the press coverage for days. Behind closed doors, though, the New Zealanders had other concerns. Harmison had made an impression as painful as it had been rapid. He had taken eight wickets for 202. He had got rid of Richardson for 93 and then crashed through the middle order in the first innings. In the second, there had been one spell when he had taken three for 14 off 19 deliveries, Richardson (101), Astle (49) and Vettori (five) all departing caught behind, with 13 of those runs coming from edges through the slips. If Geraint Jones had not spilled a simple chance off Daryl Tuffey during the same spell, Harmison would have celebrated his first five-wicket haul on home soil.

Every time New Zealand had got themselves into a position to win the game – and they were still in the hunt until the very final session – someone had stolen the initiative from under their noses. The pattern would be repeated throughout the series and, as often as not, it would be Harmison who broke their hearts.

Vaughan was back for the Second Test, but was making no promises about hanging around for the entire game. His wife was expecting their first child and he headed for the hospital as soon as the birth was imminent. For New Zealand, there were more injuries to contend with, Craig McMillan breaking a finger and Jacob Oram straining a side. Bond, worst of all, would soon be ruled out of the whole tour without featuring.

Rain allowed a mere 19 overs on Headingley's first day, reducing the drama to a single incident. Martin Saggers, once of Durham, took a wicket with his first ball in his first home Test. By the end of day two, New Zealand looked secure enough on 351 for six, but again they were pegged back each time they threatened to break away from England. Fleming, orchestrating the innings, was deprived of a century by Harmison who sent him back for 97 just after tea. It was not a one-man show – indeed, England's bowlers were hunting as a pack – but the Durham man was again the focal point as New Zealand slumped from 202 for one to 215 for four. The innings closed on 409 and England surpassed that with 526, Trescothick scoring 132, Flintoff 94 and wicket-keeper Jones 100.

Halfway through day four and New Zealand were still in the game. A few hours later they had unravelled again. By the evening Harmison, conceding less than three runs an over, as he would do all series, was bowling to five slips and a gully, with a fly slip lurking. England were playing with near-Australian levels of ruthlessness. Any chance of a final-day miracle was snuffed out with eight overs of Hoggard and Harmison. Hoggard ended with four for 75, Harmison with three for 57, and the batting side were swept away for 161. The home team settled the series by knocking off the 45 runs required with disdainful ease.

Fleming struggled to make sense of what had happened. "I would be lying if we said we weren't demoralised. We've just lost the series, despite posting 409 in helpful bowling conditions, and that's not how it should be when you bat first. It was almost as though there were two games going on out there."

The West Indians, rather than talk up their opponents, had been keen to blame their own batting for their failures in the previous series, but Fleming saw no point in pretence. "Harmison was England's leading light, no question," he said. "In these conditions, he was outstanding. He magnified all the inconsistencies in the wicket, and the pressure allowed Hoggard, Saggers and Flintoff to work away at the other end."

In that short sentence Fleming captured the essence of an England revival that would continue throughout the year. Since Sabina Park, Harmison had reinvented himself. His growing confidence in the Caribbean seemed to infuse his team-mates so that they, too, began to play above themselves. That chain reaction flooded the team with self-belief. By the New Zealand series, winning had become a habit.

Strauss had merited his man-of-the-match award at Lord's and Jones was full value for his at Headingley. Another batsman, Thorpe, would be similarly honoured in the final match. But cricket has coined a term for a player that a side turns to in times of difficulty – a 'go-to' player – and Harmison, the gawky, quiet lad with a penchant for home, had become just that in a matter of months. It could be no coincidence that his rise and that of the team coincided exactly.

Cairns echoed his captain before the series finale at Trent Bridge. Asked to explain what separated the two sides, he replied: "Purely Steve Harmison."

Richardson agrees. Indeed, as England fed off Harmison, the touring side were being ground down mentally by him. "Our batting became geared around his spells. You worried when he was coming on for his next spell and you had to work yourself up for it," says Richardson. "We ended up talking about how we were going to attack the other bowlers but they were operating well around him as the spearhead.

"We were in the games and suddenly England took them away from us. It got us down. You start asking questions about yourself and everybody looks at each other."

The final Test did not quite offer Cairns his deserved fairytale to mark the end of the all-rounder's 62-Test career. Yet again, the touring side put themselves in a perfect position on the first day, Fleming leading from the front with a century, only for Harmison to thrust out an oversized boot and kick the door back open again. From 225 for one, New Zealand slipped to 272 for four, the quick bowler taking two wickets in consecutive deliveries with the second new ball. Nathan Astle, beaten for speed, edged into his stumps and McMillan went lbw first ball. It was all so familiar.

Cairns somehow disrupted the pattern by bowling his heart out to give his side a 65-run first-innings lead, taking five wickets on his way to match figures of nine for 187. But back came England, Giles taking four wickets and Harmison and Flintoff three each as the New Zealanders crumbled to 208 all out. England needed 284 to win and Thorpe obliged with an unbeaten hundred to complete his side's first whitewash over New Zealand since 1978.

During the game Harmison had overtaken Muttiah Muralitharan as the highest wicket-taker of 2004. He ended the series with 21 wickets at an average of 22.09. Flintoff was England's next most successful bowler, with 10 wickets at 29.10.

As for Richardson, he ended the tour mentally drained and with a new medical condition. "All series, Harmison had got that extra bounce and hit me time and again above the thigh pad," he said. "I had a black and blue hip. I nicknamed it 'Harmison Hip'. A few of the others got it, too." Richardson had had a successful tour, topping the averages with 61.50.

His hundred at Lord's had been a career highlight. But the trip had taken its toll and he would call time on his playing days at the end of the same year.

"I was never a naturally talented batsman and I had to graft for runs. It takes a lot out of you mentally. I was pretty much exhausted. Harmison was a handful. I'm just glad I can say I played against him," he said.

"We had compared him with Ambrose during the trip. In a few years, I think he will be remembered as a fine bowler. He doesn't look that quick but I can tell you he's up there. I remember being impressed about the way he used his height. A lot of bowlers collapse their front leg in delivery but he didn't. He didn't sledge either. He doesn't operate like that. He just gets on with it."

Brian Lara knew the deck was stacked heavily against his squad as the West Indies arrived in England for part two of the Test Match summer. They had failed to stand up to Michael Vaughan's side in the Caribbean and been crushed, and a repeat looked on the cards. The West Indies had allowed Bangladesh to draw a match in the meantime and Sir Viv Richards soon resigned as chief selector, amid suggestions of a rift with his captain.

Perhaps it was the weakness of Lara's hand that prompted him to try a round of mind games before the return Test series. In effect, he tried to turn a 6ft 4ins negative into a positive.

Harmison, Lara declared at a news conference, was a good bowler, but what would happen if he were to break down? And where would England turn if their opponents discovered the secret to playing their strike bowler? "The more you get accustomed to a bowler, the more they peter out into something you can handle," he suggested. "I don't know if they have a Plan B."

It was a neat ruse, aimed both at ratcheting up the pressure on Harmison while belittling England as a one-man team. For all its subtlety, however, it was to backfire spectacularly.

For a while, Lara might have thought he was on to something. His side had taken some confidence from reaching the NatWest final ahead of England, even if they had subsequently been roundly thrashed by New Zealand, and they must have been encouraged by Harmison's lack of edge in the first two Tests. Unfortunately, the rest of the England team refused to comply and play like belittled men.

It had not been so long before that Harmison was suspected by some observers of being a man lacking mental and physical robustness. Now he was universally lauded. In a sense, he was in danger of becoming a victim of his own success. The better he got, the more indispensable he made himself. And, in 2004, his improvement was beginning to pay dividends not only in Tests but also in one-dayers. Despite England's messy NatWest campaign, Harmison emerged with unexpected credit. He had begun, indeed, to look like the perfect bowler, threatening at all times but also staunching the run flow with his new-found stock bowler's accuracy. He was beginning to look like a thoroughbred who also had the heart for donkey work. Vaughan, keen for England to abandon their obsession with 'bits-and-pieces' one-day all-rounders, conceded he would like to rest Harmison but felt increasingly unable to do so. "His performances in Test matches over the past six months have been special and he is just trying to get his head around the one-day game... he is undoubtedly a world-class performer now in both forms of cricket, which will be a huge bonus for us."

When the Test series began at Lord's, the pressure mounted still further on Harmison. Flintoff, one of the team's workhorses, was only half-fit and might be prevented from bowling by a bone spur problem in his ankle.

Despite that, England began perfectly after Lara, nagged by negative thoughts, put the home side in. By the end of the first day they had hammered their way to 391 for two. Strauss, excelling on his home ground again, made a century, as did his captain. By the second day Key – in the side after Butcher had suffered whiplash in a car accident while visiting his physiotherapist about another injury – had scored 221 out of England's 568, a mountain built at four-and-a-half runs an over.

With the ball in hand, however, Harmison misfired from the start. His second over went for four leg-side fours as he either dropped short or over-pitched and, clattered for another boundary by Gayle next over, he was taken off. After 20 overs, West Indies had blazed to 107 without loss.

With England's match-winner off colour, 'Plan B', it transpired, was to come in the shape of an unappreciated left-arm spinner who had taken a mere two wickets in the Caribbean.

Ashley Giles, once memorably derided as a cricketing "wheelie bin", removed Smith, Gayle and Lara for ten runs in the space of 27 balls. The next morning, he even opened the bowling with Hoggard. Finding significant turn, he finished with four wickets, the never-say-die Flintoff produced a late 13-ball burst which earned him three wickets without conceding a run, and England had bowled out their opponents for 416. Harmison, wicket-less, was hit for 72.

Giles continued the assault in the second innings with five for 81, his first five-wicket haul in a home Test, and took his hundredth wicket in the process when castling Lara with a beauty that spun through the gate. England won by 210 runs and Giles grabbed the man-of-the-match award ahead of his captain, who made two centuries in the game, and Chanderpaul, who made 128 not out and 97 not out in a losing cause.

England were as irrepressible at Edgbaston, winning the Second Test by an even bigger margin of 256 runs and, again, Plan A failed to get off the ground. Trescothick hit hundreds in both innings while Giles snapped up another nine wickets but the man of the match this time was Flintoff. His 167 first up, out of another imposing total of 566 for nine declared, included 17 fours and seven sixes, one of which, to Flintoff's delight, was dropped by his father in the crowd. Harmison, meanwhile, toiled away anonymously again, with match figures of one for 93. At least there was his batting. Sent in at number 11, he blitzed 31 not out off 18 balls, including five fours – one a reverse sweep – as well as a six off pace bowler Jermaine Lawson.

Harmison's less than scintillating form was being well masked by his team-mates, but few of them believed he had, as Lara had hoped, been 'found out'. Giles said the first two wickets had not suited the fast bowler, adding with some foresight: "With Steve's record recently, I am sure he will be keen to get a few more wickets under his belt and I think someone is going to pay the price."

England had retained the *Wisden* Trophy inside nine days. They needed another four days of play – the second day of the Third Test was washed out – to clinch the series at Old Trafford. Harmison improved in the first innings without significant reward. West Indies, indeed, held the upper hand at halfway, leading by 65 runs. Their hold on the match would have been even tighter but for a battling Thorpe's century.

The home team, however, as so often during the summer, then found a fifth and sixth gear and romped away to win by seven wickets. Flintoff, nannied as a short-burst strike bowler because of his ankle, took three wickets in each innings as well as scoring his seventh half-century in successive Tests. Lara, falling cheaply to the all-rounder in both innings, had the consolation of becoming the fourth man in Test history to reach 10,000 runs. Harmison, meanwhile, consoled himself that his rhythm was returning at last as he helped clean up the West Indies second innings for 165 by taking four of the last five wickets.

If that improved his mood, The Oval would transform it. Victory there would give the team seven Test wins in a row, a run achieved only twice before by England, the previous instance against West Indies and Australia in 1928-29 when a young Harold Larwood was beginning to make a name for himself.

England – without a single Surrey player in the ranks – batted first and set a cracking pace. Harmison, padded up, was clearly champing at the bit by the second day. At lunch, England were 413 for nine and the declaration seemed imminent. Harmison and Anderson, however, were told to go back out and swipe a few more runs. They obliged, putting on 60 at a rate of knots, Harmison blasting his best Test score of 36 not out off 27 deliveries, including three sixes in consecutive overs as he freed his arms.

His batting suggested there was nothing much wrong with his confidence and so it proved. Ball in hand and with ground to make up, he came out and produced a seven-over spell of vitriolic fast bowling. Much of the time he pitched short but his pace was so sharp and his line so good that the batsmen were repeatedly caught between pulling or taking evasive action. Gayle, fending, was caught behind in his third over and Sylvester Joseph followed three balls later as he was squared up and edged to third slip. Harmison continued to prey on the batsmen's minds, even when he was rested or during breaks in play. When he came back for a second spell, Dwayne Bravo was caught third ball off a top-edged pull. Carlton Baugh departed first ball after the next drinks break. Corey Collymore was then beaten for speed while Lara, having hit 79, tried to abort a pull as the ball climbed on him and only managed to loop to fine leg. Harmison's first spell gave him figures of 7-0-24-2. In his second he boasted 6-1-22-4 as West Indies caved in for 152 and were forced to follow on.

The drama continued unabated in the final session. With the game as good as gone, Gayle was determined to set his own agenda. Pulling and driving off back and front foot, he hit Hoggard for six fours off six balls in his second over of the innings, an unprecedented feat in Test cricket. Harmison, though, came back for a second spell. and Joseph failed to prepare himself for his very first ball, edging behind as he tried to protect his throat. It was the bowler's hundredth Test wicket and he made it 101 next over with Sarwan's scalp.

Having turned his series around, Harmison ended the day with amalgamated figures of 17-1-59-8. He had gone into the game with eight wickets from the three previous matches and series figures of 100.4-18-381-8. He would add one more wicket next day as West Indies took the game into the final session of the third day before capitulating by tenwickets.

It was England's tenth win in 11 tests in 2004. After the game, the latest player world rankings were published. Flintoff was rated the third best all-rounder. Harmison, leapfrogging Sri Lanka's Muttiah Muralitharan and South Africa's Shaun Pollock, was the world's top bowler.

The English season ended in a flurry of one-dayers. Only a short time before, Harmison would have expected a little well-earned rest and recuperation, but his NatWest showing spelt more hard labour.

England, exuding confidence, warmed up for the Champions Trophy by beating India, who were without Sachin Tendulkar, 2-1. The first game at Trent Bridge ended in a seven-wicket win and Harmison provided one of the highpoints. All-rounder Alex Wharf took three wickets in the first three overs of his international debut to all but seal the game, while Harmison almost stole the show by cleaning up the innings with a hat-trick. After a bright but wicket-less first spell, he returned to have Mohammed Kaif caught behind, driving, and Lakshmipathy Balaji caught at second slip off a lifter. Ashish Nehra then smacked the next delivery straight back into Harmison's hands.

He ended the series as England's best bowler, with seven wickets at 16.28 while conceding 4.24 per over. His one-day star continued to rise in the Champions Trophy, his eight wickets in the tournament bettered only by Flintoff, although England missed out in a dramatic, twilight final against West Indies.

England's most significant success came against the world champions in the semi-finals. Along with their Ashes woes, they had not beaten the Australians in 14 one-day starts, a run stretching back to early 1999. Ponting's team were determined not only to extend that misery but also to fill the one significant gap in their trophy cabinet, having never won the Champions Trophy.

Vaughan, though still to convince in limited-overs cricket, scored 86 and took two wickets to inspire his side to a six-wicket win. Australia's coach, John Buchanan played down the game's significance, calling it "a snapshot in time" but England did not see things that way. For them, the result highlighted the fact that they were closing the gap on the world's best side.

"The game at Edgbaston was serious; it was a really important game for us," said Graveney. "You had two dressing rooms, one side that thought they would never win and one side that thought they never lose.

"England hadn't beaten Australia for a long period of time in a meaningful contest. They had won Test matches, but only when the series had already been decided. So that was a big game. It was a slow wicket and some of their batsmen wouldn't have faced Stephen before. Even in the first few overs he made them hurry up a bit. He left his calling card."

Harmison also got caught up in a revealing confrontation with Matthew Hayden. The Australian, a towering batsman, was used to dominating his opponents and enjoyed the odd verbal joust as well. Harmison, in contrast, was known for keeping his council. His new status would have made him a prime target for Hayden. For once, though, Harmison was having none of it.

"He may not fit the caricature of a nasty, mean fast bowler but he can hold his own," says Steve Williams. "Apparently Hayden said something like: 'You're not bowling at Zimbabwe now.' Harmy said something back, then got him out soon after. Ponting came in next and, so I heard, said with a big grin: 'What did you say to Hayden? I've never seen him so angry.'"

CHAPTER FOURTEEN

AWOL

Just before setting off to South Africa in December 2004, Harmison agreed to a face-to-face interview with author and journalist Donald McRae. Working for *The Guardian* newspaper, he had been expecting to travel up to the north-east but received a late phone call suggesting a meeting at Heathrow instead, prior to the bowler's departure.

Harmison's agent, John Morris, had stipulated that Zimbabwe – Harmison had pulled out of a five-match one-day series in the country because of his moral concerns over President Robert Mugabe's administration – should not be discussed but McRae found Harmison willing to talk on all issues. It was the fast bowler's state of mind that day, however, that formed the heart of the article. Homesickness had not resurfaced as a Harmison talking point for a considerable time but here it was again suddenly, and back with a vengeance.

An airport in the run-up to Christmas, in retrospect, was an odd choice of venue for an interview. Harmison had a few hours to kill before meeting up with the England squad, but it left him at the mercy of his emotions, and without his team-mates or an England press officer as back-up. What McRae got was an interview from the heart, rather than a stage-managed PR exercise.

"Today is the day I wish I wasn't a professional cricketer," Harmison told McRae. "Today is the day I wish I worked in an office in a nine-to-five job. Today is probably the worst day I've known as a cricketer."

While McRae had clearly planned to ask Harmison about his struggle with homesickness, and welcomed the chance to meet him on his own in a surreal airport setting, he says now, "I was surprised how frank he was about his feelings. Modern-day sports people so often try to hide behind their image or clichés, but he wasn't like that at all.

"He couldn't explain why, but he said he had felt much more comfortable about going to the West Indies earlier in the year. He spoke about his family, and said if they wanted him to give up the sport, he wouldn't think twice about it. He said he inundated his wife with phone calls on days when he felt bad on tour, and thought that playing professional football would have been the ideal career for him rather than cricket, even if he had ended up playing for Hartlepool or Darlington rather than Newcastle.

"I wrote, I think, that his eyes glistened. It certainly felt like he was close to tears. He managed to control his emotions – but it was obviously a battle for him."

McRae decided to end his piece on an upbeat note, underlining Harmison's rise up the world rankings while looking forward to the 2005 Ashes. "Whatever you think about his homesickness, you could tell he is a competitor, by the way he talked," McRae said. "He was clearly motivated by playing against the Aussies." In the article in *The Guardian*, indeed, Harmison seemed to be in danger of underestimating the South Africans by suggesting they were a stepping stone to the bigger challenge ahead.

There was another quote in McRae's article, however, which caught the eye. It was a public echo of what Harmison had said in private to Hussain and some of his team-mates, just over a year before, prior to the tour of Bangladesh. Dismissing the importance of the world rankings, Harmison suggested to his interviewer that he would be satisfied with five or six more years as England's premier strike bowler.

Most sportsmen and women so revel in their successes and the accompanying adulation that they invariably overstay their welcome, embracing self-denial as their powers wane in an attempt to recreate their better days. Few find themselves able to stay true to that wisest of maxims, that it is better to retire at the top. Yet here was a sportsman apparently with one eye on the exit, barely six months after breaking into the big time.

Harmison also told McRae that regular overseas tours only added to the burden he felt as an international cricketer. "Staying at Number One is not some huge ambition," he said. "I'm more concerned with getting through these opening weeks."

There would be no grievous bodily harm in South Africa. Harmison, indeed, did not manage much actual bodily harm during the ten-week tour. He probably deserved no more than a couple of hours of community service, considering the superficial damage he caused. It was almost as if he failed to turn up at all. For GBH, read AWOL. His descent down the world rankings would be almost as surprising and as sudden as his ascent.

Harmison had been due to warm up by touring Zimbabwe but opted out of the trip on ethical grounds. Others had been expected to follow his lead in protesting against President Robert Mugabe's government but, in the end, he was the only one to make a stand. England duly went and conquered, coasting to a 4-0 one-day whitewash against the under-strength Zimbabweans.

The South African leg, however, was regarded as the serious business. For years, South Africa had been Australia's closest challengers. In 1999, they should have knocked them out of the World Cup semi-finals, only to lose their nerve on the final ball of the match. By 2005, though, the team was in transition. England were now rated as the second best side in the world and it was they who expected to win the five-Test series.

In many ways, the squads were well matched. South Africa had batting strength in Smith, Gibbs and Kallis, but England had Vaughan – himself rated number one in the world not so long before – Trescothick, the up-and-coming Strauss and Thorpe. The Pollock-Flintoff all-rounder's battle promised to be intriguing. And while South Africa boasted a proud home record – since their return from isolation, only Australia had managed to win a series there – England had the momentum of seven wins in a row.

Harmison, however, was seen as the player that separated the sides. In his absence, South Africa might have felt they had the edge in the battle for the inaugural Basil D'Oliveira Trophy. With him, England felt virtually unbeatable.

Significantly, both captains were talking about him. Vaughan was in no doubt, Harmison would be a big threat and his bowling would be a major influence. Smith suggested that South Africa might attack him from the outset. "It's important that we get him on the back foot straight away," he said. "The key factor for Harmison is confidence."

The entire touring team's confidence was to take an early blow, at the same time raising questions about the tour's compacted schedule. Originally, England had expected to play a short Test series in Zimbabwe but that had been shelved. Half a dozen of their Test side, Harmison among them, had not taken part in the one-dayers there and thus arrived in South Africa having played no first-class cricket for four months.

The five Tests in South Africa were scheduled to take place within six weeks. England would have a single first-class game to prepare and no further opportunities to put things right. They would then play seven one-day internationals in a fortnight. When England fluffed their lines badly in their opener against South Africa A at Potchefstroom, concerns over the wisdom of agreeing to such a format soon surfaced.

England were trounced by seven wickets. Harmison bowled fast, wild and too short and took two wickets, but it was the lack of form among the incoming batsmen that caught the attention. Butcher, Trescothick and Thorpe scored 23 between them over two innings. South Africa A's assistant coach Mickey Arthur observed: "The top-order definitely looks underdone... If I was Duncan Fletcher, I'd be worried." Vaughan called it a "kick up the arse" and all his players were ordered back out into the middle for extra practice as soon as the game ended. The First Test was four days away.

Ray Jennings, South Africa's coach, has a reputation as a free-thinker. It is customary to take a few speculative pot shots at opponents before the outbreak of hostilities, but Jennings played most of his mind games with his own players. The mercurial Gibbs and the outrageously gifted Kallis were his targets. Both were working their way back from injuries but Jennings seemed more concerned over their mental attributes. "Sometimes talent is over-rated. I'd rather see a guy of half the talent and double the right attitude," Jennings told the *Wisden Cricketer* magazine. "As we speak, I don't get a warm feeling that Herschelle subscribes to my vision." Kallis, he said, was coasting as an all-rounder and letting his bowling lapse. "I'm gonna turn on the heat, make or break him. No soft option. Treat people softly and they'll become soft," Jennings said. If Duncan Fletcher was tempted to mutter anything equally provocative to his players, he did so behind closed doors. If anything was said to Harmison, it did not work.

Instead, England's other summer wonder, Andrew Strauss, was left to do all the groundwork as Vaughan's side won the

First Test by seven wickets in Port Elizabeth to complete an unprecedented run of eight consecutive wins. It was also the team's eleventh Test victory in 12 starts. Strauss, South-African born, scored 126 in the first innings and 94 not out in the second. The Middlesex left-hander had played Tests against three opponents and scored centuries in his first innings against each of them. He had also scored hundreds in both his home and away debuts. He looked, sounded and behaved as if he had been born to play at the very highest level.

Harmison, meanwhile, was looking as if he had regressed into the novice he had been only 18 months previously. While Hoggard had begun the series by dismissing Smith – who had started the previous series between the sides with scores of 277, 85 and 259 – for a second-ball duck, Harmison opened with a booming wide and a first over costing 11 runs. In all, he took one for 142, his worst match return for England. In retrospect, his one wicket was huge but owed much to luck. In yet another erratic over, full of wides and ballooning bouncers, Kallis appeared to lose sight of a full toss and it cannoned into the base of his off stump before he had scored. Harmison was left to contribute with the bat. Coming in at number 11, he slogged his way to 15 off 16 deliveries, including a six off Steyn, and helped put on a valuable 67 – England led by 88 after the first innings – for the final two wickets. England's bowling hero, though, was Simon Jones who, after taking a fine catch to dismiss Smith in the second innings, removed Kallis and Pollock with consecutive balls to begin a burst of four for 14 in 40 deliveries.

Vaughan conceded after the game that England's cricket had been "quite shoddy" at times but he took strength from the fact that his side had still contrived a victory. "We felt we were at about 75 per cent," he said. Harmison – who seemed to be trying too hard, according to his captain – had not been close to that.

The next Test at Kingsmead was one of those cricketing curios – a full five-day game that ended in stalemate and yet retained all the hallmarks of a classic. In a roller-coaster encounter with a twist at every turn, England were bundled out for a paltry 139, conceded a 193-run first-innings deficit, amassed 570 for seven declared in their second visit and were only deprived of victory on the final evening by bad light. Both teams left Durban with bitter-sweet emotions. Few English commentators could recall a game of such fluctuating fortunes.

There had been a stronger look to South Africa for the game, with Gibbs back from a finger injury, left-arm spinner Nicky Boje back from surgery following thyroid cancer, and AB de Villiers inheriting the gloves from the axed Thami Tsolekile. Winning the toss, their bowlers encountered little resistance as the English tourists tramped one by one back to the pavilion. The bristling Harmison (who took three for 40 iff his first 15 overs) and Hoggard appeared to have levelled things up when the home side slumped to 118 for six in reply only for Kallis to make sense of an easing pitch with a stylish, saintly-patient 162. The next highest score was Pollock's 43.

The game swung as Strauss and Trescothick, batting again, each returned with centuries during an opening stand of 273. Thorpe also got to three figures and England declared on 570 for seven. South Africa, chasing 378 to win, were in danger of defeat on 290 for eight with only Steyn to come but were reprieved by black clouds. "I think we were a bit lucky at the end there," Smith conceded, while Vaughan said South Africa had "got out of jail".

Harmison took five wickets in the game. Statistically, it was an improvement. Yet the doubts persisted. He was still bowling grapeshot and a yard too short to threaten the likes of Kallis, who was able to leave the majority of his deliveries before punishing the odd four-ball. The wayward deliveries meant he failed to create any sort of pressure. He had begun the first innings well, roughing up Smith and getting him cheaply, but failed to capitalise. Later, even Ntini had the audacity to hit him for three straight boundaries in an over. In the second innings, Harmison removed Gibbs and Kallis for two runs within 17 balls in what would prove to be his most productive burst of the series, but was unable to press on. Luck also went against him, Geraint Jones having put Gibbs down earlier after diving needlessly across first slip. Harmison's last contribution came in the final overs when he hit Pollock on the fingers with consecutive deliveries. Pollock ended the game with bad bruising. How England must have hoped for a lucky break or two at that point.

Harmison needed a pivotal moment to his tour, just as had occurred at The Oval against the West Indies. Nothing was quite clicking, as if his arms and legs were out of time with each other. That moment seemed to come on the second morning of the third Test in Cape Town.

South Africa, having won their third toss in a row, had been held in check on the first day, chiselling out 247 for four. Kallis, the key man, was 81 not out when Harmison ran in at him.

His first ball smashed into his fingers, prompting an immediate visit from the physiotherapist. His second, a perfectly aligned bouncer, prompted Kallis to jack-knife backwards and land on his backside. The third was left outside off before Kallis's head was snapped back by a short delivery, which bucked viciously off the pitch. Visibly unsettled, the batsman played half-heartedly at the fifth ball and was beaten before scrambling a couple of leg byes off the final delivery.

It was an electric passage of pace bowling. Crucially, though, Kallis had survived and Harmison's moment – for that was all it proved to be – had gone. So had England's. Kallis responded with a masterclass of cold-blooded accumulation as he made 149 out of a first-innings total of 441. England were then routed for 163 on a blameless pitch, with Ntini taking four wickets and Charl Langeveldt, bowling with a broken left hand after being hit by Flintoff, five for 46.

For the best part of a year, England had relied on bold, aggressive and supremely confident cricket to subdue their opponents. Whenever they had flagged, a new player would step into the breach. If Harmison had been the catalyst, his team-mates had followed willingly. Man-of-the-match awards had been sprinkled about liberally, while eight different players had scored centuries in England's run of eight wins in a row. It was only reasonable to assume that it would happen again after the side had been reduced to 95 for four in their first innings. Flintoff, for one, had no doubts. "We are going to have to scrap, but we have been in this position before in the past 12 months and there is a great deal of confidence among the team that we can get back into the Test," he said. "It seems that every time we need a performance... somebody sticks their hand up and puts a special one in. Tomorrow will be no different."

That confidence was soon to sound like complacency. England came out on the third day and continued to go for their shots where a more measured, Kallis-like approach might have paid greater dividends. South Africa, 278 runs in credit, decided against enforcing the follow-on. Despite dallying over their second innings, they were soon celebrating a series-levelling 196-run victory. Comically, they were held up at the end by Harmison, who hammered a Test-best 42 not out, which included some impressive pulls and drives. There were seven fours and a six, with 18 off a Pollock over. Harmison, indeed, top-scored in the innings. The old joke – 'he could become a useful all-rounder if only he could improve his bowling' – sprung to mind.

England, for the first time in almost 18 months, were forced to take a long, hard look at themselves. The problems were easily identified. The team's big men were playing small. Two years before, Vaughan had been hailed as the world's best batsman, but in the first three Tests, his feet stuck in treacle, he had made 84 runs at an average of 14 (Strauss had scored 465 runs at 93 a visit, while even Harmison was boasting an average of 19). His second-innings dismissal in Cape Town, hooking lazily at Ntini shortly after Key had charged insanely down the wicket and been stumped, had seemed absurdly reckless. Flintoff, meanwhile, one of the world's leading all-rounders, was failing in one discipline at least, with just one half-century to his name in six visits. Harmison, the world's leading bowler a few weeks before, had taken seven wickets for 432 runs at 61.71 a shot. His wildest delivery at Newlands had gone through second slip. For *The Sun* newspaper he was now "Barmy Harmy", his mental strength under question.

Mike Procter was bemused by what had gone so wrong. "He lost his rhythm completely," he said. "Rhythm is a really difficult thing to define. It's your timing. So when you run in, you're not running in too fast but fast enough to get your deliveries going. He hits the ground quite hard when he is running in.

"It's just an amazing thing – one of those unbelievable things that happens in sport. You get a quality bowler like that and he suddenly loses it. It's like Tiger Woods suddenly not playing well. The only thing here is that it carried on for a bit too long. It never happened to me because I had a crazy action. I had to run in fast to bowl fast, with a fast arm action."

Other commentators, too, were worried. The Sky Sports team were full of sympathetic former players but they were struggling to make sense of Harmison's predicament. For Hussain, with one eye on the 2005 Ashes, questions had to be asked of all the team's leading lights.

"Some English players are happy with the level they achieve, rather than asking themselves how they can get better. That's the question that Harmison, Flintoff and Vaughan have to ask themselves," he said. "Their performances have been phenomenal over the past year but they must not think they have done enough. They mustn't rest on what they have done, it's just not enough. They should use Kallis as an example. 2004 has gone now."

Of even more concern was Cooley's imminent departure. Contracted to the Academy, the bowling coach had only been seconded to the senior team for the first three Tests. Hussain, though, pointed out that bowlers could sometimes hide behind their coaches. "Surely Harmison now knows what he needs to do to put things right," he said. Botham, his fellow commentator, responded: "I think it's like all these sports psychologists – I often wonder how many Test runs or wickets they got."

Cooley would be replaced by Mike Watkinson, who added: "I think self-belief is something with Harmy. He perhaps frets more about the game than people realise behind the scenes."

Harmison himself had few answers. "I can't put my finger on why it's not clicking. Perhaps I tried too hard at Durban and you've got to give credit to Jacques Kallis. He's the most difficult batsman I've had to bowl at because he leaves me so well."

Superior batting, indeed, had to be part of the equation. After Cape Town, Kallis had replaced Dravid as the number one batsman in the world rankings. Harmison slid to fifth among the bowlers.

England's players dispersed to lick their wounds after 15 days of cricket in three weeks. The fast bowlers, as always, were the most frazzled and frayed. Harmison managed to steal some free time with his family – his father Jimmy spends a major chunk of his annual holidays watching his son play – before they flew home after a few weeks in South Africa.

Things were not about to let up, however. There were question marks over Flintoff's fitness after a scan revealed an abdominal muscle tear. For the first three Tests, the all-rounder had papered over the bowling cracks, but now even he might be struggling. To add to the imponderables, Simon Jones had been replaced by the rusty James Anderson. South Africa, meanwhile, had recalled Mark Boucher behind the stumps. The side for the Fourth Test looked their strongest yet. The momentum, it was widely agreed, had swung decisively to the hosts.

The game would rival the Second Test in terms of excitement. A bowler with a name beginning with 'H' would play the crucial role in deciding the result, but it was not Harmison. Statistically, in fact, he had his most unsuccessful game as an England bowler. His batting, however, was another matter.

England's top-order failed to dominate in their first innings, but Strauss got significant support this time, with Vaughan beginning to dent the middle of his bat at last. Strauss made 147 on the opening day. At 227 for one, England looked pretty. Key had also answered the call with 83. His departure led to a slump, though, and honours were even at 263 for four at the close. Vaughan, scratching about at the start of his innings like a man with a bad skin condition, somehow survived.

Next morning, following delays for rain and murky light, England's middle order vanished without trace, Thorpe failing to score and Flintoff making two, but the England captain bloody-mindedly played himself into form. He found a vital ally in Giles, who helped put on 51, but the touring side still looked vulnerable at 329 for eight.

Harmison was next in. Logically, his confidence should have been shot. After a year of heading the English attack, he was now being carried by his team-mates. Unlike Vaughan, he simply could not find his way out of the maze. It must have crossed his mind that any other bowler in the team would already have been dropped, had they duplicated his figures for the first three Tests. He had become so peripheral a figure that the South Africans probably did not think him worth sledging.

Within the hour, though, they were probably cursing both his parentage and his progeny. With Vaughan now approaching his best form, the pair put on an unbeaten 82 in just under 15 overs by the close. The previous highest partnership for England's ninth wicket in South Africa was 71, by Harry Wood and Jack Hearne in 1891-92.

If Harmison was nervous at the start of his innings, he did not show it for long. Soon he was playing out a maiden to Pollock, then to Ntini. A lofted straight drive for four off Kallis followed, a trick he repeated against the exasperated Ntini. Vaughan decided to stop protecting his partner as the runs flowed. "I asked him: 'Are you confident to play?'" Vaughan said later. "And he said: 'Yeah, give me as much strike as you want.' He's a funny batter. He always says if he gets past the first three balls, he's in. I usually need 100 balls."

In the next two overs, Vaughan scored two and Harmison 16, all in fours. He had reached 30 not out when the day ended, South Africa's fielders rather than England's batsmen accepting the bad light, to howls of derision from an elated Barmy Army. No one knew it at the time, but Vaughan and Harmison's partnership would exceed England's eventual margin of victory.

Harmison, of course, would have exchanged all of those

runs for a single wicket, but by now he simply could not get a sniff of one. With bad light delaying the next morning, Vaughan opted to declare on the overnight 411 for eight, hoping to capitalise on the conditions. Immediately, however, the sun broke through. Gibbs prospered, ending the day undefeated on a century. Harmison, meanwhile, totally unable to find his line, was taken off after just two overs with the new ball. He improved on his return, cutting one ball back through Gibbs, which just cleared the stumps, but by his thirteenth over he had pulled up with a calf strain and was forced off the field.

Gibbs was eventually dismissed for 161 and South Africa edged in front after the first innings. Hoggard took five wickets but said afterwards that it had been his worst bowling of the tour. Flintoff, in Harmison's absence, was forced to grimace through 30 overs.

England ended the fourth day on 197 for five, 189 ahead, with Trescothick on 101 not out. Two results still seemed possible – a South African win or a paint-drying draw. Trescothick, however, egged on by Giles, launched a murderous assault on the final morning, plundering 180 in all as England added a further 135 at 7.5 runs an over.

The fun really started when Harmison came in at the fall of the eighth wicket. Trescothick immediately hammered a six and two fours off Boje's next over and continued in the same vein against all comers, hitting his last 52 runs, containing five fours and four sixes, off 32 balls. Harmison contributed three not out to the 58-run ninth-wicket stand, as England declared on 332 for nine. The game seemed destined to end in a stalemate, but, by the ninth over of South Africa's second innings, the equations were being reformulated yet again. The home side, needing 324 to win in just over two sessions, started without their captain, who was still groggy after being struck on the head by a ball in one of Jennings's famously rigorous fielding drills. Soon they were 18 for three, after Hoggard flattened Rudolph's stumps with a pearling inswinger and Kallis edged to slip next ball. Bizarrely, Harmison, despite his sore calf, was bowling with some consistency, and even had a routine catch dropped by Vaughan at leg gully during the innings. But Hoggard was unstoppable. By tea he had taken the first five wickets to fall. He added a sixth shortly after the break, Giles got Gibbs for 98 and then Flintoff smacked Pollock on the helmet before snaring him in the same over. It was left to the haystack-haired Hoggard, a man as averse to the limelight as Harmison and who is happiest doing the team's "donkey work", to win the match by 77 runs in the sixtieth over. Hoggard finished with career-best figures of seven for 61 and 12 for 205 in the match, England's best since Botham's 13 for 106 against India in 1979-80.

Smith, who had come in against doctor's orders at number eight, made a courageous 67 not out, but was reduced to the match notes, as was Harmison. For the first time in his Test career, he had failed to take a single wicket. He seemed to have lost all feeling for his bowling action. "The trick is how often you are away from that zone or feeling, and how readily you can reclaim it," said Cook. "I suppose people like McGrath click regularly. With Stephen, you wonder if the psychological factors are so great that he finds it difficult to re-click."

Yet at least Harmison had found a way of contributing. Tailenders are judged primarily by contributing to partnerships rather than scoring individual runs, their priority being to survive while allowing specialist batsmen to dominate the strike at the other end. At The Wanderers, Harmison made 33 runs in the game without being dismissed but, critically, shared in two stands that added 140 runs – almost one-fifth of England's total runs in the Fourth Test.

In the true tradition of lies, damn lies and statistics, indeed, Harmison could have argued that he was now playing as a batsman who bowled a bit, with an average of 29 with the bat (as well as the best scoring rate in the team, with seven runs from every ten balls he faced) and 61 with the ball.

England's 2-1 series triumph, their first in South Africa for 40 years, was all but assured when the first day of the final Test at Centurion was lost to rain. South Africa raised home hopes on the final day but England steadied their collective nerve to draw. Harmison, again, bowled a mixed bag of the unplayable, the unreachable and the unspeakable to take two wickets. What luck there was went against him. In the first innings he induced an early edge from Gibbs but the chance was dropped. The same happened with de Villiers when he had made 34 of his 92 runs. With luck, Harmison could have finished the series with around 14 wickets. He had more catches – five clear chances – grassed than any other bowler. Instead, he ended with nine at 73.22 runs apiece. Fortunately for England, Hoggard (26 at 25.5), Flintoff (23 at 24.95), Jones (15 at 26.66 in four matches) and Giles (11 at 40.81) made up for him.

Harmison's wretched tour, however, was not finished. Flintoff, so often his close support, flew home for ankle surgery after the Tests but Harmison was retained, despite being unavailable for most of the seven one-dayers because of his calf strain. Some observers thought he was being kept with the party not so much because of his likely contribution to the one-day campaign, but because England wanted to oversee his rehabilitation while bluntly making the point that Harmison could not come and go as he pleased.

When he did return to the fray for the fourth one-dayer, he was as unsuccessful as ever, hoiked for 65 runs off 10 overs for Gibbs's wicket. Axed, he was brought back as injury cover for the last game of the series and took one for 55 off 10.

South Africa, inspired by Justin Kemp's powerful batting, dominated England – despite South Africa-born Kevin Pietersen's equally hefty blade – and cruised to a 4-1 victory.

Harmison caused his biggest stir in South Africa in the final days.

In an interview with a handful of journalists, he said that he wished he could have gone home after the Tests. Those present read it as a throw-away remark, made half tongue in cheek, rather than a plea. His comments, however, were interpreted differently by others in the travelling media and given greater emphasis. Passing a fitness test on his injured leg before the one-dayers had been like "a kick in the teeth", he was reported as saying, adding: "Everybody knows I would go home at any time. If you had offered me the chance to go home, I would have gone but that is just me and my character."

In truth, Harmison was only echoing what he had said many times before, namely that he lives with his homesickness. Whenever he is playing badly, however, such talk is translated into sacrilege. It was neither surprising nor sacrilegious to those around him in the England set-up, however. It was part of the Harmison contract. It was blunt, straight-down-the-line honest. It was not particularly helpful, but it was Harmy.

Vaughan, interviewed at the end of the tour, was adamant. "I wouldn't even consider not having him in the team," he said.

CHAPTER FIFTEEN

A PARADOXICAL HERO

In March 2004, England's long-suffering fans had fallen into a trance of delicious disbelief. For 20 years, since the glory days of Botham and Willis, they had waited for a match-winning bowler. Now they scratched their heads and wondered how it was possible that Steve Harmison could bowl so majestically. By early 2005, they were asking exactly the opposite question.

His extraordinary 12-month rise seemed to have been mirrored by a sudden and equally improbable collapse. Nobody had seen him coming at Sabina Park and no one had predicted his South African slump either.

Why did it happen? Was his homesickness, held in check in Australia, Bangladesh and the West Indies, somehow to blame? Was his very character fundamentally flawed? Had he crumbled under the pressure of growing expectation, been found out by top-class batsmen, or had he simply mislaid the magic?

Harmison had been widely regarded as the foundation of English ambitions to topple Australia as the best side in the world, so the issues were certain to get a full airing. Perhaps it was a mix of all those factors. Certainly his miserable departure from Heathrow did not suggest a robust athlete invigorated by the challenge ahead.

Former England batsman and captain Brian Close, unashamedly old school, is one to suggest that Harmison lacks mental fibre. "He shouldn't go (abroad) if he can't handle it," he said. "I can't remember anyone getting homesick in my day. We used to set off in September for our tours to Australia and get back in late April." Close, the man who took West Indian bouncers full on the chest without blinking, adds: "We used to have a phrase, 'leave the wives at home and bring the Ashes back'. Now they even get their wives out there. I used to love touring and seeing the world and I did it for the honour."

He is in the minority, however. Those closer to Harmison see things very differently. For them, the gulf between his home and away personae is likely to remain a factor, but it is not an issue. Where once he might have retreated, they say, he now bites the bullet and boards the plane. He still frets, but he bowls. His performances in Bangladesh and West Indies also proved beyond doubt that his is a talent that can travel.

Harmison is, of course, certainly an oddity, perfectly designed physically for his chosen trade but peculiarly unsuited emotionally. He is, in effect, an international talent with a parochial perspective. He has matured but the facts remain the same – Harmison would still prefer to have been a footballer and would still prefer to stay home. In a modern world where so many people of little or no talent seem to be obsessed with chasing fame, he stands out as an individual with huge talent who could do without the recognition (not unlike Jackie Milburn, indeed). He loves cricket the game but baulks at cricket the life. That may be a flaw. As Hussain points out, however, that does not make Harmison so different from many other leading sportsmen and women. "To reach the top there is generally a character flaw in most people because they have had to sacrifice something to get there," Hussain argues. "People's motives are not all the same either."

In other ways, Harmison has a perfect attitude. Once comfortable within a group and once at the end of his bowling run-up, he will run through walls for his team. He will bowl and bowl and bowl, with a calf strain if necessary. He will put everything into his batting even when his bowling confidence is so fragmented that he feels like giving up. It is that old-fashioned honesty which makes him so popular with fellow players.

Hussain accepts that "if you are slightly off, if you are homesick, then it is going to affect your performance" but does not see that problem effacing what Harmison can offer. "There is never a question on the field of him saying : 'I don't want to bowl, I'm homesick.' Perhaps his percentages are down a little, he's at 90 per cent because he's feeling a little homesick. But I have never heard him say that he didn't want to play or bowl."

In truth, his homesickness has become a red herring. It is a fact and it is unlikely to go away. England, though, like Durham before them, have accepted it, even if they find it hard to comprehend. They work around it as best they can. Vaughan, Fletcher and the selectors know there may be Harmison low points, as in South Africa, but there have already been unsurpassed highs. The media, however, craves stories on a daily basis and they know Harmison's is there to be refashioned when things go less well for him. When Harmison was taking seven for 12, his mental make-up could be humoured and ignored. When he had taken nine for 659 on the High Veldt, however, it was less worthy of such tolerance.

Geoff Cook, a man who has known Harmison from the very start, stands squarely in the big man's camp.

"Physically, his homesickness can be debilitating," agrees Cook. "I have never come across anybody who has had it like Stephen. I don't know if having his family there would make things easier. I think it's the environment in Ashington he enjoys.

"But I have lots of admiration for Stephen. He still goes out there to perform. People call him fragile but there is a paradox there. He has a fantastically strong mentality to get where he has, but he's delicate at the same time. He's not quite an anti-hero, yet he's not your traditional hero. But for me what he has done is certainly heroic, because he has put the English team on the map. I think he is a hero because what he does is so exciting. He bowls fast and aggressively and gets good batsmen out. It's a very undressed heroism, based purely on his talent and performance.

"To his credit, although he still likes being in Ashington, he sees being away from home as very much part of what he wants to be – the top bowler in the world. For people to say he is weak is to get the wrong end of the stick completely. I think he is very, very strong.

"Consider the quips and comments people make. To ride above those, to lose your run-up in Perth in front of all those people, to come through all that to become the world's top-ranked bowler shows unbelievable strength of character."

Most commentators in South Africa agreed implicitly with Cook by looking elsewhere for the causes of Harmison's difficulties. Hussain does wonder whether Harmison's meteoric rise has subconsciously undermined his performance, since he clearly does not hanker after the trappings of success. "He would quite like, I think, to come home for two months and shut the doors, wherever he lives, and say: 'I don't want to know about how I'm bowling, or my lengths, I want to do what I enjoy doing.'" But Hussain and most experts feel the fundamental factor was a technical, rather than a mental, failing.

In Kallis and Gibbs, of course, Harmison came across astute, world-class batsmanship. Against the very best, indeed, he has everything still to prove. He has taken nine Australian Test wickets at 50.55 apiece, and 18 South Africans at an average of 59.55, compared to his overall Test average of 28.66. But his control was lamentable against every single batsman he came across in South Africa, not just Kallis and Gibbs. No one needed to knock him out of his stride, as Smith had planned, because he never got into it.

Bob Willis, England's last eminent fast bowler and now a respected broadcaster, believes the problems stemmed from England's failure to manage their prize asset before the South African series. He backs the team's system of central contracts but believes players are not monitored closely enough.

"I know for a fact that Errol Alcott, the Australian physiotherapist, insists that their players bowl once a week, no matter how long the break between games, to make sure they keep their bowling muscles working and keep in rhythm," says Willis. "It's surprising, but I don't think England did that with Stephen and he looked particularly out of synch and ended up bowling the wrong length the whole time. He knew he was doing it but he couldn't do anything about it. I think that was the key thing."

Harmison had bowled sparingly in the indoor nets at Durham in the run-up to the tour, instead concentrating on strength and fitness during another six-week spell at Newcastle United. It was not exactly a crime. "Crickey, if someone had said a few years ago that Harmy's mistake was that he was in the gym!" adds Hussain. "It's not the worst mistake, it's not as if he was sitting on the sofa."

That gym-only regime, though, which had worked before the West Indies tour, did not work a second time. Willis says both England and Harmison must learn those lessons. "These are now highly paid professional performers and one sometimes gets the impression that they are left to their own devices," he says. "That simply won't do in modern professional sport. Stephen obviously lives a long way north and it may be highly inconvenient for him to come to Loughborough once or twice a week, but that is what needs to be done. It shouldn't be a hardship at all."

England's tight schedule in South Africa also worked against Harmison. He has always been regarded as a rhythm bowler, requiring frequent workouts to keep his action well oiled. His decision to boycott the Zimbabwe series meant he had little time to find his feet. In the West Indies, more time had been available.

Harmison, in public at least, has remained sanguine about his struggles. Interviewed after the South Africa Tests, he said it was just a matter of him bowling himself back into rhythm. Catches hadn't stuck, he said. "I'm not too disappointed. I had a good year and this one has started less well. It's swings and roundabouts."

Hussain is also confident that his former team-mate will bounce back, although he stresses that Harmison will need to repay the faith invested in him in kind.

"With Steve Harmison you do go the extra yards. England have gone up to number two in the world – why have they done that? Because of Steve Harmison and Andrew Flintoff, simple as that. Harmison gets it right and England win eight Tests in a row – it coincides perfectly," says Hussain.

"It's like Australia without Warne or McGrath. They're three-quarters of the side, or half of it. Last time we beat Australia, in Sydney, there was no Warne and no McGrath. They were characterless by comparison.

"You go the extra mile for Steve but, in all honesty, if he wants to maintain the standards that he has set, he has to go the extra yard as well, as he did at Newcastle, which was perfect for him.

"Form comes and goes. You can't play at your best all of the time. That is true of all athletes. He needs to work out where he is going to be in the cricketing world. It might not necessarily be number one, he might not necessarily get 70-odd wickets in a year again, but he must sense his own goals and he has got to get back to where he was technically. He has gone backwards.

"But England must not constantly ask why is he not number one in the world, or why is he not getting seven wickets. He might just get three but he will still be what we need. If he gets back to a stable platform, he might have the odd winter where he bowls like he did in the West Indies.

"Duncan Fletcher has backed Steve Harmison right the way through. If Harmy is going to go that extra yard, he should do it to repay Fletch. If he is going to put in that extra fitness work or those extra bowling sessions or try to get over his homesickness, it should be for Duncan, because Duncan has backed him through thick and thin."

For some, though, South Africa, that stepping stone to the Ashes, left one nagging question mark hovering in the air.

Willis was among many onlookers surprised by Harmison's failure to bowl himself into form at some stage during the series. Mike Procter was another. "It is hard to get your head around it, it went on for a long time," he said. "It is hard to see it happening to someone like Shaun Pollock. It is a worry."

Could it be that Harmison might turn out to be a man blessed by those fickle sporting gods for an agonisingly limited period, before being cast back into the ranks of mere mortals? There have been such examples before. Swing bowler Bob Massie's star had risen and fallen even more dramatically in the early 1970s, the Australian taking eight wickets in each innings of his debut against England only to be dropped after six Tests. Another Australian, Gary Gilmour, took six for 14 in the World Cup semi-final against England and five for 48 in the final against West Indies but only played five one-day internationals in a disappointingly truncated career.

Willis hopes that Harmison, "a very fit young man and very committed to the England cause", will rediscover the magic at Durham. He wishes he would be less candid about his homesickness – "He needs to get this off his CV. It's just the sort of thing that the Australian psychology machine will home in on. He really needs to put the lid on that, otherwise it's going to come back and haunt him" – and he prays he will dismiss the doubters with an emphatic return.

But he adds: "The thing that one fears is that the form that we saw from Steve in the West Indies and in England might have been a blip on the monitor.

"I wish I were more confident. He obviously has all the attributes to do the job and we've seen him do that job. Although the West Indies were a weak side and the New Zealanders are in decline in the Test Match arena, you don't get wickets in the West Indies on those pitches unless you can bowl. If you look back through England history, it is only really Trueman, Snow, Fraser and Harmison who have had success as pace bowlers in the West Indies. That should give him all the confidence to come back and reinvent himself.

"He was number one in the world. The litmus test will be whether he has the nous, commitment and skill to get back there."

APPENDIX

47 ALL OUT
(OVER-BY-OVER COMMENTARY FROM SABINA PARK – MARCH 14TH, 2004)

1st over: Hoggard.
2 runs. Bowling over the wicket to the left-handed Gayle from the Blue Mountains End, Hoggard targeted the batsman's off stump while shaping the ball into him. Occasionally, he pushed a delivery across him. Gayle played two of the six deliveries, clipping the fifth off his legs for two runs to Harmison at fine leg. He almost did not get that far, however, offering no stroke to the fourth delivery, which swung back and missed his off stump by a fraction. Score: 2-0. Hoggard 1-0-2-0.

2nd over: Harmison.
Maiden, but a flattering one. Harmison, from the Headley Stand End, loosened up against Smith with two express bouncers in his first three deliveries. Smith, however, did not have to play at a single ball, the last of which sent Read diving down the leg side. Umpires discuss the light. Score: 2-0. Harmison 1-1-0-0.

3rd over: Hoggard.
6 runs. He began the over with an lbw shout against Gayle

but the ball was probably missing leg. The next delivery took an inside edge, squirting out to Michael Vaughan at square leg. The batsman responded by chopping two past point, then driving a leg-stump inswinger through mid-on for four. Score: 8-0. Hoggard 2-0-8-0.

4th over: Harmison.

4 runs. Harmison managed two deliveries before play ended for bad light after 3.2 overs, but both suggested better things to come, the first a better line and length to which Smith shouldered arms, and the second which hurried the batsman and beat him outside off. West Indies 8-0, still 20 adrift. Play resumed the next morning at 9.35a.m. in bright sunshine. Collingwood substituted for Butcher. Smith was forced to play two balls out of four, edging the last one for four to third man. Score: 12-0. Harmison 2-1-4-0.

5th over: Hoggard.

Maiden. Hoggard bowled over the wicket at Gayle, shaping the ball into the left-hander from an off-stump line. Gayle was forced forward throughout as Hoggard looked for swing. Gayle was offered one scoring chance when Hoggard's third ball began on leg stump and swung away but the batsman flicked and missed. The fourth kept the batsman honest, going straight across him without swing. Gayle played at each ball apart from the fourth. Score: 12-0. Hoggard 3-1-8-0.

6th over: Harmison.

Maiden. Harmison, bowling slightly shorter than Hoggard and still bowling in the low 80s as he began to get into his rhythm, allowed Smith two defensive back-foot blocks before his third delivery exploded off a length. Smith, rooted to the crease, was beaten. He shouldered arms to the fourth, even quicker delivery as it fizzed through to Read. The fifth ball, slower and wider, was wasted. The sixth ball, like the fourth, threatened but was well left. Score: 12-0. Harmison: 3-2-4-0.

7th over: Hoggard.
1 run. Hoggard erred on leg stump again with his first ball but Gayle flicked, missed and was hit on the pad. The second ball, straight across and too wide, provoked a flat-footed front-foot flash, which missed. Gayle, with soft hands, dabbed the next ball into the covers to steal a single. Smith then easily left a straight ball angled across him. The fifth ball was on a perfect line and length with a hint of inswing, Smith pushing off the front foot into the covers, before the left-hander was beaten by the last ball, swinging back inside his bat and clipping his front pad, producing an appeal first from Read and then, in reaction, Hoggard. Score: 13-0. Hoggard 4-1-9-0.

8th over: Harmison.
Wicket maiden. Gayle, facing Harmison for the first time in the innings, lasted four balls. Jumping into the air as he played back, he managed to leave the first. The second reared up and hit him on the left bicep as he was squared up. The third, pitched up on leg stump, rapped his pad before Gayle flailed off balance at the next delivery, just back of a length. The first attacking shot of the day, it sailed head-high to Thorpe at third slip. Gayle made 9 off 25 balls. 13-1, West Indies still 15 behind, 9:52a.m. Ramnaresh Sarwan's first ball was short, wide and wasted but the next reared up and forced the batsman to snap his head back to avoid it. Score: 13-1. Harmison 4-3-4-1.

9th over: Hoggard.
Maiden. Another fine Hoggard, increasing the pressure.

The first delivery was a perfect line and length, Smith coming forward and prodding to cover. The second, on leg stump, was miscued off the inside edge and trickled to mid-wicket. Smith left the next going across him, the next died off the pitch to provide an easy leave, and the batsman then went back to play out to cover before another good leave, a few inches outside off stump. Score: 13-1. Hoggard 5-2-9-0.

10th over: Harmison.
Wicket maiden. Sarwan hopped off the ground to play to cover. The next ball, timed at 86mph, was played down at his feet, while the right-hander then shuffled across his stumps and pushed across the line to dab to the leg side. Sarwan opted for a little gardening after ducking under a bouncer before falling to the last ball of the over, jumping back and across and being rapped on the pad around the knee roll. Never getting off strike against Harmison, he made an eight-ball duck to complete a pair. 10:02a.m. Score: 13-2, still 15 runs behind. Harmison 5-4-4-2.

11th over: Hoggard.
1 run. Hoggard drifted another delivery into Smith's pads and he clipped it for a single to Harmison at fine leg. Chanderpaul got forward to full pitches facing the second and fourth balls, playing the rest of the over from the crease, barely getting forward. Score: 14-2. Hoggard 6-2-10-0.

12th over: Harmison.
1 run, 1 wicket. Smith shouldered arms to the first delivery and, tucked up, turned the next to short square leg. The next ball, a similar delivery, was gloved for a single. Chanderpaul dropped his hands to a short ball aimed at his body and was hit on the armguard. Crab-like, he shuffled back to the next,

his bat face closed, and the ball ran from bat through his legs and onto his leg stump, removing the bail. He made a seven-ball duck, facing two deliveries from Harmison, who celebrated with a big jump in the air, a huge grin and high fives all around. 15-3. 10:12a.m. Lara survived the final ball of the over with an extravagant backward defensive. Score: 15-3. Harmison 6-4-5-3.

13th over: Hoggard.
1 run, 1 wicket. Smith, with the most authoritative stroke of the day, drove at Hoggard only for the ball to clatter into the stumps at the non-striker's end. Next ball his inside edge passed between him and the stumps to fine leg for a single. Lara pushed his first delivery to extra cover but then took a blow on his damaged finger. He pushed forward again, slicing the fifth ball to point. Squared up on his back foot by the sixth ball, he jabbed and edged to Flintoff at second slip, who moved right to take the catch two-handed. 10:18a.m. Lara made a five-ball duck. Score: 16-4. Hoggard 7-2-11-1. West Indies had lost four wickets for four runs in nine overs lasting 43 minutes.

14th over: Harmison.
5 runs. Smith played the first ball down, safely but off a thick edge, the ball bouncing in front of Ashley Giles at fourth slip and going through for four. He then got struck on the hand as he struggled to evade a ball heading for his rib cage. The next delivery began on leg stump and cut across a nervous Smith, going through to the keeper. The next was too short to threaten and Smith ducked. The fifth was wide and short and an easy leave, and the batsman then stole a quick single with a back-foot block to cover. Score: 21-4. Harmison 7-4-10-3. Harmison's most expensive over.

15th over: Hoggard.
2 runs, 1 wicket. Smith kept out a good blockhole ball, missed a leg-stump inswinger and then, failing to get to the pitch, mis-hit a drive back to Hoggard, who instinctively took the catch. 21-5, West Indies still seven runs behind. Smith made 12 off 42 balls. 10:25. Jacobs flicked his first ball off a thick inside edge to square leg for two, survived an lbw shout (the ball was clearly missing off) and then blocked a forward defensive to cover. Score: 23-5. Hoggard 8-2-13-2.

16th over: Harmison.
Two runs. Harmison's first ball, around 90mph, was just back of a length and left by Hinds. The next, on the same length, whistled past Hinds's left shoulder as he played back. Hinds then check-drove the third delivery through mid-on for a couple. He then fenced and missed at a rearing delivery, provoking a half-appeal, pushed the next to point and then turned away from a bouncer. Score: 25-5. Harmison 8-4-12-3.

17th over: Hoggard.
8 runs. Hoggard beat Jacobs with his first ball as he prodded forward but, seeking more swing, he overpitched the next and the wicket-keeper drove it through mid-on for four, the shot of the morning. Those runs put West Indies one run ahead. Jacobs, standing a foot outside his crease, left a tired ball angled across him, blocked the next to short leg and then drove on the up and in the air through mid-off for another boundary. Hoggard finished with a rapid ball across the left-hander, who offered no stroke. Score: 33-5. Hoggard 9-2-21-2.

18th over: Harmison.
Maiden, 2 leg byes. Harmison began with a wasted, wide delivery across Hinds, then pitched up and beat him with his

next delivery as Hinds drove. The batsman left a short ball, also wasted, and was then hit on the pad with a leg-cutter, prompting a strangled appeal. Hinds missed a fuller fifth delivery, flicking to leg, but ran two leg byes. Harmison switched to round the wicket and Hinds blocked off the back foot. Score: 35-5. Harmison 9-5-12-3.

19th over: Simon Jones.
6 runs. Jones, replacing Hoggard at the Blue Mountains End, greeted Jacobs with a bouncer. The batsman then blocked a short ball before picking the next up off a good length and hitting four through mid-on, the ball striking the boards on the first bounce. He flicked the shorter fourth ball off his hip for a single to Harmison at fine leg. Hinds blocked off the back foot, was beaten as he stayed rooted to the crease, and played and missed with a drive. Score: 41-5. Jones 1-0-6-0 (1nb).

20th over: Harmison.
Maiden. Jacobs leant back to avoid Harmison's first ball and then turned away from the next to be struck on the back of the right shoulder. Unnerved by the short ball, he lashed out at the next, his powerful cut dropped by substitute fielder Paul Collingwood at gully after getting both hands to the chance. Jacobs dropped a short ball to his feet, played a tired delivery to gully with ease, but then lashed out again, heaving across the line to a ball not short enough to pull. It missed the stumps and went through to Read. Score: 41-5. Harmison 10-6-12-3.

21st over: Jones.
Maiden. Hinds began with a back-foot block, then drove loosely and edged just short of Graham Thorpe at third slip, who parried the ball. Hinds then blocked on the back foot

again before playing forward and edging, along the ground this time, to Thorpe. He ducked under a bouncer before playing back to another ball on the stumps. Score: 41-5. Jones 2-1-6-0 (1nb).

22nd over: Harmison.
Double wicket maiden. Jacobs, flicking to leg, struck on the pads. Harmison then produced a good bouncer at Jacobs's head. Next ball the batsman, again fearing a body blow, gloved straight up in the air and Hussain ran behind the stumps from short leg to take the catch, 41-6, 10:59a.m. Jacobs 15 off 22 balls. Eight close catchers for Tino Best – four slips, a gully, point, short leg and leg gully – with one fielder out. Harmison's next delivery took off, Best just getting out of the way. He flinched at the next ball, turning his eyes away, and snicked behind. 41-7, 11:02a.m. Best two-ball duck. Five wickets for Harmison. Adam Sanford came in and edged a routine chance to Thorpe at third slip, who put it down. Score: 41-7. Harmison 11-7-12-5.

23rd over: Jones.
1 wicket, 2 runs. Hinds flicked a leg-stump delivery for a single and Sanford, after a back-foot block, dug a blockhole ball off leg stump for another fine-leg single. Hinds drove at the next ball and was caught behind, 43-8. He made three off 23 balls. 11:08a.m. Jones then cut a ball back off the pitch, going through Corey Collymore's defences and over the stumps, then produced a sharp lifter, which Collymore evaded. Score: 43-8. Jones 3-1-8-1.

24th over: Harmison.
Wicket maiden. Sanford went back to a lifter and let it go through. Harmison then produced a short and wide delivery, the worst of his spell. The third ball was much too good for

Sanford to get a touch. Harmison now had a six-man slip cordon, a fly slip 20 yards off the third-man boundary, point, with short leg the only man in front of square. Another ball was left, then Sanford, wafting without moving his feet to a good-length ball, edged to Trescothick at first slip, 43-9, 11:14a.m. Sanford made one off eight balls. Score: 43-9. Harmison 12-8-12-6.

25th over: Jones.
4 runs (2 leg byes). Corey Collymore and Fidel Edwards both ran leg byes before Collymore ended the over with a slog, which went for two into the covers. Score: 47-9. Jones 4-1-10-1.

26th over: Harmison.
3 balls, 1 wicket, 0 runs. Harmison tried a slower ball, which Edwards hit into the ground, the ball flying to the slips. Harmison beat the edge with his next ball, then squared up Edwards with the third delivery, the ball flying to Trescothick at slip. Edwards made a seven-ball duck. 11:20a.m. Score: 47 all out, 25.3 overs. England required 20 to win. Harmison 12.3-8-12-7.